FOCUS GROUPS
Second Edition

Applied Social Research Methods Series
Volume 20

APPLIED SOCIAL RESEARCH
METHODS SERIES

Series Editors

LEONARD BICKMAN, Peabody College, Vanderbilt University, Nashville
DEBRA J. ROG, Vanderbilt University, Washington, DC

FOCUS GROUPS
Theory and Practice

Second Edition

David W. Stewart
Prem N. Shamdasani
Dennis W. Rook

Applied Social Research Methods Series
Volume 20

SAGE Publications
Thousand Oaks ▪ London ▪ New Delhi

For information:

 Sage Publications, Inc.
2455 Teller Road
Thousand Oaks, California 91320
E-mail: order@sagepub.com

Sage Publications Ltd.
1 Oliver's Yard
55 City Road
London, EC1Y 1SP
United Kingdom

Sage Publications India Pvt. Ltd.
B-42, Panchsheel Enclave
Post Box 4109
New Delhi 110 017 India

Printed in the United States of America

Library of Congress Cataloging-in-Publication Data

Stewart, David W.
Focus groups: Theory and practice / David W. Stewart, Prem N. Shamdasani,
Dennis W. Rook. —2nd ed.
    p. cm. — (Applied social research methods series; v. 20)
Includes bibliographical references and index.
ISBN 0-7619-2582-1 (cloth: alk. paper) — ISBN 0-7619-2583-X (pbk.: alk. paper)
    1. Focused group interviewing. 2. Social sciences—Research—Methodology. 3. Social groups. I. Shamdasani, Prem N. II. Rook, Dennis W. III. Title. IV. Series.

H61.28.S74 2007
300.72′3—dc22   2006009180

This book is printed on acid-free paper.

06   07   08   09   10   10   9   8   7   6   5   4   3   2   1

Acquisitions Editor:	Lisa Cuevas Shaw
Editorial Assistant:	Karen Greene
Production Editor:	Diane S. Foster
Copy Editor:	Robert Holm
Typesetter:	C&M Digitals, (P) Ltd.
Proofreader:	Andrea Martin
Indexer:	Molly Hall
Cover Designer:	Candice Harman

Contents

Preface to First Edition

In late 1986, when we were asked to write a book on focus groups for the Sage series on Applied Social Research Methods, there were few extant sources on the use of focus groups. There were a few collections of readings and some chapters in various handbooks, but these tended to be either dated or quite superficial, and Merton and Kendall's (1946) classic, "The Focussed Interview," was long out of print. By the time we completed the book in late 1989, numerous treatments of the conduct and application of focus groups had appeared. Most of these books were by experienced focus group moderators and provided considerable detail about the recruitment of focus group participants, the actual conduct of groups, and the interpretation of data generated by focus groups. We have referenced a number of these books in our own monograph, and we feel that the reader will find them useful supplements to the material we offer.

Despite the recent appearance of other books on the topic, we feel that our own work offers a unique perspective on focus groups. Our original intent—and we think we have adhered to it—was to produce a relatively short volume that provides a simple guide to the conduct and application of focus groups and places the use and interpretation of focus groups within a theoretical context.

Focus group research had its origins in early research on group dynamics, persuasive communication, and the effects of mass media. These origins and the rich empirical and theoretical foundations they provide are infrequently acknowledged and used. We have revisited the origins of focus group research in our text and have tried to tie focus group research more closely to its origins in mainstream social science. In doing so, we believe we have set our own book apart from others on the same topic that tend to provide considerable detail on the conduct of groups, as well as detailed examples, but tend to place less emphasis on the theoretical dimension.

The reader will find three chapters are especially concerned with the theoretical dimensions of focus groups. Chapter 2 draws heavily on the literature of group dynamics and the social psychology of groups. Focus groups are, by definition, an exercise in group dynamics, and the conduct of a group—as well as the interpretation of results obtained from focus groups—must be understood within the context of group interaction. Chapter 4 considers the literature on interviewer and moderator effects, including the interaction of group and moderator. This chapter not only emphasizes the importance of the moderator in determining the quality of focus group data but suggests that the data are themselves the result of a unique interaction of moderator and group. Only an understanding of this interaction and the factors that contribute to it provides a sound basis for the interpretation of focus group data. Chapter 6 also includes some discussion of the theory of content analysis. Because this chapter is concerned with the interpretation of focus group results, it seemed particularly appropriate to treat the theoretical underpinnings of this interpretation.

The remaining chapters of the book, as well as portions of the chapters already discussed, are devoted to the mechanics of designing, conducting, and interpreting the outcome of focus groups. We hope the result is a balance of theory and practice that suggests that focus groups need not be ad hoc, atheoretical, or unscientific exercises. Rather, we have tried to convey the notion that focus groups can be useful social science research tools that are well grounded in theory.

No work is ever the sole accomplishment of its authors. Ours is no exception. We would be remiss if we did not acknowledge the contributions of others. Len Bickmann, coeditor of this Sage series, was instrumental in encouraging us to undertake the project. Tom O'Guinn of the Department of Advertising at the University of Illinois reviewed an earlier draft of the manuscript and offered a variety of helpful criticisms and suggestions. Siony Arcilla typed the final version of the manuscript. To all of these individuals we extend our gratitude. Any remaining problems and points lacking in clarity are, of course, our responsibility and exist despite the generous help of others.

David W. Stewart
Prem N. Shamdasani
November 1989

Preface to Second Edition

When we began work on the second edition of this book, it became evident to us that many dimensions of the focus group environment, as well as the underlying methodology itself, had evolved significantly since we wrote the first edition. We believe this evolution has been a positive force and has both expanded the range of problems and settings for which focus groups are appropriate and improved the general practice of conducting focus group research. Among these trends in focus group research are the following:

1. A very significant acceleration of the diffusion of focus groups into the behavioral and health sciences
2. The globalization of focus group research
3. The consolidation of focus group facility ownership with a consequent increase in advertising by owners using a diversity of advertising appeals
4. The growth of niche positionings among focus group facilities and moderators with specialists emerging to focus on specific ethnic groups, particular age ranges, and specific industries, among others
5. The emergence of creative innovations in focus group design and the use of technology. These innovations include virtual focus groups that bring people together via Internet or videoconference, the use of natural groups (as opposed to the use of groups of strangers), and the conduct of focus groups in the home or office where the natural environment can serve as a stimulus for discussion

At the same time these positive trends have occurred, there has been growing criticism of focus groups among the traditional heavy users of them—the marketing community. The trade and academic literature criticizes focus groups for a multitude of shortcomings: their use as an inappropriate substitute for quantitative research and in-depth individual interviews; their use as an evaluative research tool rather than an exploratory tool for discovery; and the conduct of "cookie cutter" groups conducted by relatively unskilled moderators. Although we believe there is some merit in this criticism, it is our view that such criticism is not so much about focus group methodology as about the manner in which the methodology is sometimes employed. Even the best of tools will not yield good results when used inappropriately. A hammer is very useful for driving nails but is a poor substitute when the need is to cut a two-by-four in half. A hammer can certainly be used to break a two-by-four in half, but the result is neither pretty nor especially helpful. The same may be said of the focus group: It is a useful tool for some types of research problems but neither pretty nor helpful in all research contexts.

One of our objectives in writing this book was to better define the research contexts and problems for which focus groups are best suited. We also wanted to provide practical advice about how to design, implement, and interpret focus group research. We did not, however, want to write just another "how to" book—there are many available. Rather, we sought to show how focus groups fit into the broader fabric of research in the social and behavioral sciences. In doing this, we also sought to move focus group research from a tool principally used by marketing researchers to a tool more broadly applied. We were gratified to find that the first edition of this book found a broad audience in the social, behavioral, and health sciences, as well as among marketers.

In this second edition, we have retained our attention to focus groups as a general research tool for the social sciences. We have also attempted to remain close to original source materials when appropriate. Focus group research is a mature methodology, and much that is today considered "best practice" has its origins in earlier work. At the same time, we have updated the book to reflect the positive evolutionary trends in focus group research. We have also added a third author to expand the experience base and perspectives.

We would be remiss if we did not thank the many readers of the first edition who have offered us numerous suggestions and thoughts over the years. Our students and our research clients have also challenged us to better explain the role of focus group research as a social science research method and to help improve the general level of research practice revolving around focus groups. Finally, we thank the editors of this series for inviting us to write the first edition, encouraging us to develop a revised second edition, and offering helpful and constructive comments about how the book could be improved.

David W. Stewart
Prem N. Shamdasani
Dennis W. Rook
January 2006

1

Introduction

Focus Group History, Theory, and Practice

Among the most widely used research tools in the social sciences are group depth interviews, or focus groups. Originally called "focussed" interviews (Merton & Kendall, 1946), this technique came into vogue after World War II and has been a part of the social scientist's tool kit ever since. Focus groups emerged in behavioral science research as a distinctive member of the qualitative research family, which also includes individual depth interviewing, ethnographic participant observation, and projective methods, among others. Like its qualitative siblings, the popularity and status of focus groups among behavioral researchers has ebbed and flowed over the years, with distinctive patterns in particular fields. For example, in qualitative marketing studies, the use of focus groups has grown steadily since the 1970s, and today, business expenditures on focus groups are estimated to account for at least 80% of the $1.1 billion spent annually on qualitative research (Wellner, 2003). Also, focus groups no longer solely involve small research projects that rely on two or three groups. Airbus, for example, conducted over 100 focus groups all over the world to assist the development of its new superjumbo jet (Emerson, 2000).

In sociology, arguably the first field to embrace group research, qualitative research flourished through the 1950s, faded away in the 1960s and 1970s, and reemerged in the 1980s. Various patterns of focus group ascendance, decline, and revival characterize other fields, yet it seems reasonable to conclude that focus group research has never enjoyed such widespread usage across an array of behavioral science disciplines and subfields as it does today.

The diversity of research purposes, theories, and procedures that characterize the behavioral sciences suggests that focus groups will materialize differently in different fields. This, in fact, is the case, and it speaks to the versatility and productivity of focus group research. What is problematic with focus group research today, as anthropologist Grant McCracken observes, is an intellectual climate that reflects "substantially more concern with practice than theory" (1988, p. 15). This is particularly the case in marketing research, where dozens of articles and books tend to emphasize the do's and don'ts surrounding the myriad of executional details involving recruiting participants, preparing discussion guides, selecting moderators, blocking time slots, inviting observers, ordering food, analyzing data, and preparing reports. As Rook (2003) recently observed, the stage management aspects of focus groups often preoccupy researchers to the extent that more basic issues are barely considered. In practice, researchers rarely step back to ask why they want to conduct research with groups rather than individuals, and why in a mirrored room instead of a natural setting? Answers to these and other questions can be found in closer examination of the nature and conduct of focus groups within the behavioral science disciplines from which they emerged.

BORDER CROSSINGS: THE BEHAVIORAL SCIENCE ORIGINS OF FOCUS GROUPS

For over 80 years, researchers in numerous behavioral science disciplines (both basic and applied) have relied on focus groups as a source of primary data. The fields that have—at various points in time—embraced research with groups include education, sociology, communications, the health sciences, organization behavior, program evaluation, psychotherapy, social psychology, gerontology, political science, policy research, and marketing. The core concerns of these disciplines are obviously quite diverse, which suggests that focus groups are likely to be designed, fielded, and analyzed from very different perspectives and with different priorities. In other words, the underlying conceptual domain of any field influences how its researchers select samples and construct questions and how moderators probe responses and manage interactions among focus group participants.

The inevitable impact of substantive theory on research practices stands in contrast to a tendency today to generalize a one-size-fits-all approach to using focus groups. This chapter seeks to examine the relationships between focus group theory and practice by identifying their primary historical sources and characterizing their prototypic research designs, which tend to vary dramatically according to their disciplinary origin.

As noted earlier, the lineage of focus group research is most commonly and directly traced to 20th-century studies of persuasive communications and the effects of mass media that were conducted in the early 1940s. Table 1.1 provides a summary timeline of the development of group interviewing as a research tool with a particular emphasis on its evolution within the field of marketing research. Yet this is only part of the story, as today's focus groups also evolved from two additional primary sources: (a) clinical psychological

TABLE 1.1
Milestones in Focus Group Research

1913	Strong, E. K., Jr., "Psychological Methods as Applied to Advertising," *Journal of Educational Psychology, 4,* 393–395.
1925	Poffenberger, A. T., *Psychology in Advertising.* Chicago: A.W. Shaw.
1926	Bogardus, E. S., "The Group Interview," *Journal of Applied Sociology, 10,* 372–382.
1931	Moreno, J. L., *The First Book on Group Psychotherapy.* New York: Beacon House.
1934	Lazarsfeld, P. F., "The Psychological Aspects of Market Research," *Harvard Business Review, 13* (October), 54–71.
1937	Lazarsfeld, P. F., "The Use of Detailed Interviews in Market Research," *Journal of Marketing, 2* (July), 3–8.
1940–1945	"Focused Interviews" (both group and individual) conducted by Lazarsfeld's associates Hadley Cantril, Gordon Allport, and Robert Merton, initially for CBS radio program research, later for military training and morale films.
1944	Edmiston, V., "The Group Interview," *Journal of Educational Research, 37,* 593–601.
1946	Merton, R. K., & Kendall, P. L., "The Focussed Interview," *American Journal of Sociology, 51,* 541–557.
1947	Dichter, E., "Psychology in Marketing Research," *Harvard Business Review, 25,* 432–443.
1948	Lewin, K., *Resolving Social Conflicts.* New York: Harper.
1949–1953	Trade press cites numerous uses of focus groups by advertising agencies in New York, Philadelphia, and Chicago.
1954	Smith, G. H., *Motivation Research in Advertising and Marketing.* New York: Advertising Research Foundation.
1962	Goldman, A. E., "The Group Depth Interview," *Journal of Marketing, 26,* 61–68.
1976	Bellenger, D., Bernhardt, K., & Goldstucker, J., *Qualitative Research in Marketing.* Chicago: American Marketing Association.
1979	Higgenbotham, J. B., & Cox, K. (Eds.), *Focus Group Interviews: A Reader.* Chicago: American Marketing Association.

(Continued)

TABLE 1.1 (Continued)

1982	Fern, E. F., "The Use of Focus Groups for Idea Generation: The Effects of Group Size, Acquaintanceship, and Moderator on Response Quantity and Quality," *Journal of Marketing Research, 19,* 1–13.
1990s	Books on focus groups by Stewart and Shamdasani (1990); Templeton (1994); Greenbaum (2000); Morgan (1998); Edmunds (1999); Krueger and Casey (2000); Fern (2001)
Late 1990s	Criticism of marketing focus groups appears in the trade press (Kaufman, 1997)
2003	Ethnographic influences emerge in the use of focus groups conducted in natural settings with real social groups (Wellner, 2003)

uses of group analysis and therapy and (b) sociological and social psychological studies of group dynamics. Also, there was much interdisciplinary collaboration in the early days, as well as the migration of researchers from one field (e.g., clinical psychology) to another (marketing research). Consequently, the theoretical underpinnings of focus groups emerged from what pioneer Alfred Goldman described as a "rich stew of socio-psychological and psychotherapeutic traditions and techniques" (A. E. Goldman & McDonald, 1987, p. 3).

However, a stew is not necessarily a melting pot, and fundamental differences exist between sociological, social psychological, clinical psychological, and marketing research concerns. The focus group pioneers were hardly single-minded, and marked differences of opinion and approach reflect distinctive intellectual priorities within each parent discipline. These divergent orientations toward research conducted in group settings contribute to often sharp disagreements about how focus groups should be used, designed, and fielded. This has also produced, over time, hybrid forms of focus groups whose design reflects varying degrees of sociological and psychological influence. The following discussion examines the origins and uses of focus group research in its three parent disciplines.

Contributions From Sociology and Social Psychology

Not surprisingly, sociology's core interest in social groups and group behavior led many researchers to employ group interviews in their research. Both Karl Mannheim (1936) and E. S. Bogardus (1926) report using group interviews in the 1920s. Since then, qualitative sociologists have used focus groups to study a myriad of group behavior topics, including social interaction patterns and personal space; group composition, cohesiveness, decision making, and productivity; and conformity, leadership, and social power. Sociologists and social psychologists share many common research interests, although the latter tend to focus on the individual rather than the group as the unit of analysis.

The most prominent early social psychological uses of focus groups sought to achieve understanding of the effects of media communications (e.g., radio broadcasts, government fund-raising appeals, and World War II military training films) and the underlying factors that explained the relative effectiveness and persuasiveness of a particular communication. The most famous and influential impetus to the growth of focus groups sprang from network radio researchers' frustration with their inability to diagnose why different programs received different likeability scores. Thus, the "focussed" group interview had its origins in the Office of Radio Research at Columbia University in 1941 when Paul Lazarsfeld invited Robert Merton to assist him in the evaluation of audience response to radio programs.[1] In this early research, members of a mass media studio audience listened to a recorded radio program and were asked to press a red button when they heard anything that evoked a negative response—anger, boredom, disbelief—and to press a green button whenever they had a positive response. These responses and their timing were recorded on a polygraph-like instrument called the Lazarsfeld-Stanton Program Analyzer (a recording device that is quite similar to devices still in use in media research today). At the end of the program, members of the audience were asked to focus on the positive and negative events they recorded and to discuss the reasons for these reactions (Merton, 1987).

After the outbreak of World War II, Merton applied his technique to the analysis of Army training and morale films for the Research Branch of the U.S. Army Information and Education Division, which was headed by Samuel Stouffer. This experience resulted in the publication of a paper outlining the methodology (Merton & Kendall, 1946) and eventually a book on the technique (Merton, Fiske, & Kendall, 1956). Research findings based on use of the technique, both during the war and later at Columbia University, formed the basis of one of the classic books on persuasion and the influence of mass media (Merton, Fiske, & Curtis, 1946).

Merton later adapted the technique for use in individual interviews, and in time the method, both in group and in individual interview settings, became rather widely disseminated and used. It also tended to change as researchers began to modify procedures for their own needs and to merge it with other types of group interviews that did not include the media focus procedure employed by Merton. Thus, what is known as a focus group today takes many different forms and may not follow all of the procedures Merton identified in his book on "focussed" interviews.

Ironically, focus groups soon fell out of favor in both academic social psychological and communications research as the fields adopted more experimental and quantitative approaches. However, the theoretical influence of phenomenological sociology (A. Schutz, 1967) and a revival in the 1980s of sociological interest in qualitative research methods contributed to the reemergence of focus groups, which caused some observers to conclude incorrectly that they represented a "new tool" for qualitative sociological research (Morgan & Spanish, 1984). More recently, focus groups have experienced a revival in audience reception and media research (Lunt & Livingstone, 1996). Also, focus groups have become an increasingly popular data collection method in the social and health sciences and in evaluation research (Kidd & Parshall, 2000).

Contributions From Clinical Psychology

Uses of focus groups in psychotherapeutic research emerged from the quite different priorities of clinical diagnosis and treatment. Some of the earliest clinical uses of groups date back to Moreno's (1934) seminal work with psychodrama and play therapy. Compared with groups conducted in the social psychological tradition, the clinical approach is more likely to emphasize interactive group discussions and activities; individuals' deeply seated thoughts and feelings; and extensive, wide-ranging, and spontaneous expressions. Researchers influenced by the psychotherapeutic school tend to favor focus groups that are more developmental in orientation and design. Such groups place less emphasis on evaluative tasks and tend to use more indirect ways of asking questions. Also, in contrast to individual patient-therapist psychotherapy, the interactions among participants in clinical group therapy facilitate individuals' treatment processes.

An enduring heritage of focus groups' clinical psychological origins lies in today's cadre of focus group moderators with professional backgrounds in traditional psychotherapy, particularly those forms with early-20th-century European origins (Kassarjian, 1994). The earliest and most renowned pioneer, who migrated from clinical psychological to marketing research, was Paul Lazarsfeld's student Ernest Dichter. Although he tended to prefer individual over group interviews, his consulting company trained a large number of the first generation of focus group researchers. Alfred Goldman is prominent among the second generation of researchers who transitioned from clinical to marketing research uses of focus groups, and his article, "The Group Depth Interview," is widely considered a definitive classic (1962). Many moderators today also have specific ties to newer psychotherapeutic techniques such as encounter groups, transactional analysis, and gestalt therapy, as well as sensitivity training.

Contributions From Marketing Research

The successful uses of focus groups in evaluating World War II morale and training films did not go unnoticed by the marketing research community. The procedures developed by Lazarsfeld and Merton were imported directly into CBS's research of pilot radio and television programs and are still used today. Although it is likely that some business studies used focus groups in the 1930s (Henderson, 2004), their popularity grew dramatically from the 1950s onward (Leonhard, 1967; G. H. Smith, 1954).

Marketing researchers quickly discovered the versatility of focus groups in addressing numerous concerns related to designing products and services: obtaining consumers' perceptions of prices, brands, and retail environments and their reactions to advertising and other marketing stimuli. Also, there is some speculation that, in the days before the rise of commercial interviewing facilities, interviewers grew weary of lugging around heavy reel-to-reel tape recorders for capturing their in-home conversations with consumers and responded positively to the idea of sitting down to interview a group of housewives in someone's family room. In comparison to statistical research, focus groups are more user friendly, and they can be fielded and analyzed relatively quickly. They also provide an office getaway that is often social and entertaining, as well as insightful.

Perhaps the most compelling quality of focus groups is their delivery of "live" consumers for observation by marketing managers. As Axelrod exclaimed in 1975, focus groups provide managers "a chance to experience a flesh and blood consumer" (p. 6). In many ways, market research uses of focus groups reflect both social and clinical psychological traditions, to varying degrees. Their initial emergence in the marketing literature is strongly linked to the "motivation" researchers of the 1950s (G. H. Smith, 1954), who typically had intellectual grounding in Freudian and neo-Freudian thought. Groups conducted in this tradition tend to share the exploratory, interactive, playful, and confrontational qualities of clinical psychological groups. By contrast, focus groups rooted in social psychological thinking tend to be more evaluative in purpose, direct in questioning, and lower in respondent interaction. Such focus groups are often heavily involved in gathering consumers' reactions to product concepts, marketing communications, and competitive brands.

The intellectual distinctions between the two schools are largely below the surface and tend to emerge in vague notions about what "scientific" research is and what falls short. Actually, many marketing researchers today are unaware of these historically competitive ideologies, having learned focus group practice through the oral traditions and research manuals of ad agencies, marketing research companies, and client organizations. The resulting focus group hybrids reflect varying degrees of psychotherapeutic and social psychological influence, however unconsciously. Overall, this is probably a positive development. Focus groups that rely too heavily on individuals' evaluations and voting tend toward superficial faux surveys, and ones that rely entirely on unstructured and indirect questioning may not yield sufficiently definitive findings.

Separation of Practice From Theory

Despite these differing orientations toward focus groups, it is important to recognize that the fields that have contributed most to focus group theory and practice actually share several common and basic theoretical positions about the technique's purpose, nature, and structure. Unfortunately, the core theory governing focus group research, which connects both the social and clinical schools of thought, is largely ignored and often violated by today's small army of focus group users, practitioners, and facilitators. Sometimes the consequences of this are minimal, and a focus group muddles along, yielding sufficient answers to key questions. However, most research seems governed by the garbage-in-garbage-out rule. A focus group that is designed and fielded completely at odds with the method's core logic is likely to generate questionable results. The premise of this chapter is that greater awareness of focus group theory per se will encourage researchers to design studies in ways that improve the likelihood of discovering things that are more interesting, useful, and valid.

FOCUS GROUP THEORY

This begs the question: Are there core elements of focus group theory that are common across the various disciplines that use focus group research? The answer appears to be yes, although the presence of any particular element will vary according to the research context. The following discussion proposes four normative criteria that constitute a prototypic focus group. This analysis draws heavily on both the seminal work of sociologist Robert Merton and the thinking of market research pioneer Alfred Goldman, whose ideas both integrate the social and clinical psychological traditions and bridge academic and practitioner perspectives. Stripped down to its basics, the theoretical pillars of focus group research are reflected in the (paraphrased) title of Goldman's (1962) classic article, "The [focused] Group Depth Interview."

Focused Research

In a fascinating intellectual retrospective over 40 years after his groundbreaking group studies of radio broadcasts and army morale films, Robert

Merton (1987) reflected on the historical continuities and discontinuities of focus group research. He explained that the basic purpose of the "focussed" interview (his preferred spelling) was to gather qualitative data from individuals who have experienced some "particular concrete situation," which serves as the focus of the interview (Merton & Kendall, 1946, p. 541). Interestingly, Merton explains his view of the "focussed" interview as a general qualitative research approach that can be used in both individual and group interviews. The objective of studying and learning about a "particular concrete situation" implies that an interview, whether individual or group, will be relatively singular in focus. This element contrasts with the typical uses of survey research to gather statistical measures of numerous topics and variables, and this is why focus groups are commonly prescribed for research that is either exploratory, clinical, and/or phenomenological (Calder, 1977).

Numerous published reports of focus group research in the behavioral sciences suggest that most conform to the criteria of focus. In the health sciences, for example, focus groups have been used to explore the role and concept of the nurse practitioner, social service concerns of women infected with HIV, and doctor-caregiver relationships. Sociological and social psychological studies have used focus groups to explore the lifestyles of working class Latina women, the psychosocial aspects of widowhood, and various specific aspects of interpersonal group dynamics and influences. Much clinical psychological group research maintains focus due to the common practice of including individuals whose "particular concrete situation" center around the same psychological condition. In marketing research, focus groups are used extensively to explore consumers' lifestyles and trends; their involvements in product categories and with competitive brands; and their consumption histories, aspirations, and concerns. Although many studies are relatively singular in focus, others are dispersed across a potpourri of loosely or unrelated topics, questions, and tasks (Rook, 2003). Such out-of-focus groups arise from managers' pragmatic concerns about research time and money, as well as their generally diminished interest in theoretical and methodological subtleties. Although focus groups that have multiple foci may yield information that assists managerial decision making, they are unlikely to generate the social atmospherics that are conducive to the traditional normative criteria of conversational interviewing, in-depth data elicitation, and within-group interaction.

Group Interactions

A second signature aspect of a focus group is the objective to better understand the group dynamics that affect individuals' perceptions, information processing, and decision making. The main logic for conducting the research in a group rather than an individual setting is to allow observations of how and why individuals accept or reject others' ideas. Also, stimulating interactions among group participants are hypothesized to generate more information than individual interviews would provide, although there is little support for this position (Fern, 1982). Three key research design elements directly affect the nature and quality of the interactions among focus group participants: group composition, interpersonal influences, and research environment factors. Numerous behavioral science studies have investigated these group behavior influences, and they are summarized in Chapter 2, "Group Dynamics and Focus Group Research," so the discussion here is limited to a few issues.

Merton (1987) concludes correctly that many focus groups are "not . . . groups in the sociological sense of having a common identity or a continuing unity, shared norms, and goals" (p. 555). He recommends that these nongroups should more properly be called *groupings*. On the other hand, focus group research in sociology, clinical psychology, and the health sciences is likely to gather groups comprised of individuals who do share some common identity and goals, as well as some common "concrete situation." In comparison, focus groups in marketing are far more likely to be populated with "groupings" of individuals who share a few common demographics and product usage patterns.

In the real world, marketing communications and influences filter through individuals' everyday interactions with family members, friends, neighbors, coworkers, and other social networks, yet researchers all too rarely tap these natural, existing, and accessible groups. Instead, they tend to rely on the convenience of professional recruiters' extensive lists of willing focus group participants. There may be a countertrend emerging—perhaps reflecting the growing presence of consumer ethnography—in recent reports of focus groups conducted with real groups (incoming college freshmen from the same towns) in natural settings (their homes), which helped with the design of Target's Todd Olham Dorm Room product line (Wellner, 2003).

A major issue in group dynamics research is the influence of group members' demographics, personality, and physical characteristics. Although the findings are not conclusive, they seem generally to favor the idea that groups that are relatively homogeneous are more productive and "work better." One problem with this notion is the fact that many studies were conducted 30 or more years ago when including Hispanics among a group of white respondents, for example, might have made both participants feel uncomfortable. Arguably, Americans are more comfortable with diversity today, so earlier conclusions may be time bound. Finally, there is a widespread but rarely articulated assumption that focus groups should be pleasant experiences and conflict should be avoided. This is certainly not the situation in clinical groups, with their varying emphases on confrontational encounters among group members and techniques designed to surface deep-seated emotions. Focus groups in marketing typically avoid conflict that might arise from differences in participants' age, social status, and even gender. Researchers prefer groups that are homogeneous with respect to these criteria, yet many marketing problems span these respondent characteristics. For example, a brand that is perceived as "too feminine" (e.g., Zima) might learn a lot by fielding groups comprised of both men and women. Similarly, a brand that is perceived as "too old" (e.g., Cadillac) might obtain useful information by conducting focus groups with baby boomers and both their parents and children.

In-Depth Data

A main thread that connects the diverse family of today's focus group users and providers is a belief that live encounters with groups of people will yield incremental answers to behavioral questions that go beyond the level of surface explanation. Clinical psychology is rich with qualitative research tools and techniques such as projective methods and group involvement techniques that elicit the emotions, associations, and motivations that influence particular behaviors. Focus groups in the health sciences often address emotional, even life-and-death issues. Market researchers have similar, although generally less serious concerns about identifying the underlying behavioral factors that account for consumers' attitudes, preferences, and motivations. In the 1950s, this similarity of objectives stimulated marketing researchers to adapt projective and other qualitative methods for their purposes. So many "deep" insights were published that historians have described this period as marketing's "motivation research" era (G. H. Smith, 1954).

In their early days in marketing research, the prototypical focus group was characterized by a relatively small number of loosely structured questions that center on a focal topic or stimulus and encourage extensive discussion and probing. Carl Rogers's work on nondirective interviewing was particularly influential, and many prominent focus group moderators had graduate degrees in clinical psychology or in related fields (e.g., Ernest Dichter, Ted Nowak, Perham Nahl, George Horsley Smith, Steuart Henderson Britt, Thomas Coffin, Alfred Goldman, and Irving White). Over time, focus groups have drifted away from their original emphasis on achieving in-depth consumer insights. Robert Merton's own impression of focus groups in marketing concludes that they are "being mercilessly misused" (1987, p. 557). Two factors have contributed to the decline in focus group depth.

First, focus group discussion guides tend to include too many questions, which often makes the experience more like a within-group survey than an interactive discussion. Veteran focus group analyst Naomi Henderson (2004) estimates that in comparison with the early focus groups, today's cover nearly twice the material in the same time. Rook (2003) quantifies the interaction between the number of questions in the discussion guide and the focus group length. It is common today to have 30 or more questions, which can reduce the response time per respondent to 13 seconds or less. In these circumstances, the moderator is likely to feel hurried and unable to probe interesting or unclear responses, all of which militate against achieving in-depth information.

A second problem emerges from the tendency to use exclusively direct questions and verbal responses to them. This not only is inconsistent with the historical nature of focus groups, but it also defies current scientific under-standings about the workings of the human mind. Zaltman's (2003) recent compilation of neuroscience findings concludes that the vast majority of human thought is visual, metaphorical, and emotional and resides deeply in neurological substrata. Access to these mental zones typically requires more subtle, indirect approaches to asking questions; and it suggests using nonver-bal techniques that involve visualizations or role playing. Some marketing pro-fessionals have begun to recognize the problem, as reflected in the humorous title of a *Newsweek* article, "Enough Talk" (Kaufman, 1997).

Humanistic Interview

The history of focus group theory and practice is part of the larger history of qualitative research in the behavioral sciences. In comparison with most quantitative research, qualitative research is a contact sport, requiring some degree of immersion into individuals' lives. This and its emphasis on meaning rather than measurement have contributed to its characterization as "humanistic" research. This is not meant to ennoble qualitative research; rather, it simply points to a general orientation that includes empathy, openness, active listen-ing, and various types of interactions with research participants. Clinical psy-chological groups exhibit these qualities, and arguably, focus group research in the health sciences *is* noble in its providing a voice to marginalized groups such as AIDS patients.

Focus groups in marketing tend to perform less well on the humanistic cri-terion. This is partly due to the tendency to use research more for evaluative than developmental purposes (Zaltman, 1989). Marketers have a voracious appetite for obtaining consumers' evaluations of new product concepts, adver-tising copy, and competitive brands. This is understandable and necessary, but such interests might be better served through survey research rather than focus groups. Also, groups that are dedicated to evaluative polling tend to exhibit characteristics of a "business meeting" (Agar & MacDonald, 1995) in which moderators misguidedly seek to achieve group consensus. Another factor that is likely to diminish a group's humanistic qualities is the erroneous but widespread belief that the moderator should ask every question that appears in the discussion guide, which often "destroys the elements of freedom and variability within the interview" (McCracken, 1988, p. 25).

The criticism of focus group research in marketing has been growing for a decade, and some companies (Yahoo!, AOL) have abandoned them almost entirely in favor of research alternatives such as ethnography, which facilitate greater immersion into consumers' lives (Kiley, 2005). The controversy peaked recently when Malcolm Gladwell in his best-seller *Blink* (2005) characterized focus groups as generally useless. He reiterated and elaborated his view as a keynote speaker at the American Association of Advertising Agencies' summer conference and caused quite a stir because ad agencies are extremely heavy users of focus groups (Pollack, 2005). The ebb and flow of focus group research across and within various disciplinary fields—and the attendant intellectual elements of thesis, antithesis, and synthesis—make focus groups an interesting and dynamic arena that continues to merit further consideration.

PURPOSE OF THE BOOK

Despite its widespread use, the focus group has been the object of rather little systematic research, particularly in recent years. A number of how-to books have appeared recently (Fern, 2001; Greenbaum, 2000; Krueger & Casey, 2000; Templeton, 1994), but they tend to deal with the practical aspects of recruiting and running focus groups. None reflect recent advances in the use of computer-assisted content analysis techniques that may be helpful for analyzing focus group–generated data, and few seek to integrate the focus group technique with the rich literature on group dynamics from which the method sprang. Stewart and Shamdasani (1997) and Calder (1977) have reviewed the use of focus groups in marketing, and the American Marketing Association has published collections of readings on the technique (Bellenger, Bernhardt, & Goldstucker, 1976; Higgenbotham & Cox, 1979). Morgan (1996, 1997, 1998) and Morgan and Spanish (1984) provide an introduction to the use of focus groups in sociological research. Wells (1974) offers a helpful introduction to the technique, and the Qualitative Research Counsel of the Advertising Research Foundation (1985) has published a discussion of issues and recommendations concerning the use of focus groups. Although all of these sources are useful, they are often incomplete, particularly for the student or scholar seeking a theoretical foundation for the approach.

The objective of this book is to provide a systematic treatment of the design, conduct, and interpretation of focus group interviews within the context of social science research and theory and the substantial literature on group processes and the analysis of qualitative data. Much is known about the interaction of small groups and about the analysis of qualitative data. It is on this knowledge that the validity of the focus group interview as a scientific tool rests.

PLAN FOR THE BOOK

The remaining chapters of this book deal with specific aspects of the design, use, and interpretation of focus groups. One of the important advantages of focus groups as a research tool is the fact that a substantial body of research and theory exists with respect to behavior in groups. The field of social psychology, and particularly the subfield of group dynamics, provides a strong foundation on which to build valid and useful focus groups. Chapter 2 synthesizes this literature and provides an overview of the theoretical and empirical foundations of focus group research. It considers such topics as power, leadership, interpersonal communication, social facilitation and inhibition, and the influence of group composition. The literature related to each of these issues is briefly reviewed and the implications for designing and conducting focus group research are discussed. Chapter 3 presents an overview of the basic elements and issues involved in focus group research, including the various applications of focus groups, their relative advantages and disadvantages, and the main steps in the design and use of focus groups.

Next, we turn to the more detailed mechanics of designing, conducting, and interpreting focus groups. Chapter 4 considers the problem of recruiting participants for focus group sessions and designing the interview guide. Issues related to the determination of the sampling frame, the use of incentives, scheduling, and physical facilities are considered in this chapter. Chapter 4 also addresses the problems associated with the recruitment of special groups of individuals, such as business executives, working parents, physicians, and children.

The key to obtaining rich and valid insights through the use of focus groups is an effective moderator. Chapter 5 deals with the characteristics of effective focus group moderators. This chapter summarizes the rich literature on interviewing skills and techniques and leadership styles, and it relates the relevant findings to the focus group setting. In addition to characteristics specific to the interviewer, Chapter 5 considers the potential for interaction between various interviewer characteristics and the dynamics of the group. The implications of such interactions for the quality of data obtained from focus groups are also discussed.

Techniques and approaches for conducting a focus group are treated in Chapter 6. Methods for drawing out respondents, for probing for additional information and clarification of responses, for dealing with domineering or reticent respondents, and for facilitating discussion are reviewed. In addition, the chapter deals with such topics as how to deal with sensitive or potentially embarrassing issues, how to present stimulus materials, how to deal with specialized populations, such as children, and the special issues associated with conducting groups in an international venue. The use of audio and video recording equipment is considered in the chapter, as well as the collection of observational data to supplement verbal responses. Finally, Chapter 6 considers the issues associated with conducting virtual focus via telephone, video-conference, and the Internet.

Focus groups generate verbal and observational data. The data must generally be coded and analyzed by means of content analysis. Chapter 7 provides an overview of the content analysis literature and its application to focus group data. The chapter also offers a discussion of various computer-assisted approaches to content analysis and the implications of recent research in cognitive psychology on associative networks for the analysis and interpretation of focus group data. In addition to considering the issues of content coding and analysis, the chapter discusses the interpretation of such coding and analysis.

Chapter 8 is designed to tie together all of the preceding chapters through more detailed examples of the uses of focus groups. These examples include a discussion of the problem that precipitated the research, the reasons a focus group is appropriate, the development of the interview guide, and the conclusions drawn from the focus group and the actions that followed from these conclusions. In Chapter 9, we discuss other group research techniques such as synectics, brainstorming, and the Delphi technique. Finally, in Chapter 10, we offer a brief summary of the role focus groups play in the broader array of research tools within the social sciences.

CONCLUSION

In examining the historical origins of focus group research in the behavioral sciences, one is struck by the high level of interdisciplinary collaboration and creativity. The now famous studies of World War II training and morale films were led by individuals with backgrounds in social psychology, experimental psychology, and sociology. Similarly, market research uses of focus groups were strongly influenced by the intellectual border crossings of clinical and social psychologists into the marketing field. In looking at focus group practice across various disciplines, one can also observe how group research formats and approaches vary according to the core issues that characterize a particular field. Finally, it is interesting to consider the degree to which focus groups conform to the historical normative criteria discussed in this chapter. In some cases, this merely reflects the necessities of adaptive use in a particular field or for a specific research purpose. In the worst cases, a drift away from historical focus group theory and research design norms results in focus groups that have little singular focus, elicit superficial consensual data, rarely achieve in-depth understandings, and end up as group surveys rather than qualitative interviews.

REVIEW QUESTIONS

1. What are the origins of focus group research? Why is the group interview an appealing method of data collection?

2. Why did much of the early development of focus group research reside in the study of communications? Is there something about the group interview that makes focus groups especially useful in such a context?

3. What disciplines have contributed to the development of modern focus group practice? What have been the unique perspectives and contributions of these fields to focus group practice?

4. Why has the popularity of focus group research waxed and waned over time?

5. What are some of the problems associated with the conduct of group depth interviews?

Exercise: Do a search of the Internet using *focus group* as the search term. Note the types of applications of focus group research you find. Compare and contrast these applications in terms of the research questions, sample, and approach. What does this comparison suggest about focus group research?

NOTE

1. See Merton (1987) for an interesting recollection of these beginnings, as well as how "focussed" interviewing lost its second *s*.

2

Group Dynamics and
Focus Group Research

Focus groups are inherently social phenomena, and it is important to understand the complex and dynamic social context in which group interviewing takes place (Hollander, 2004). A primary difference between focus group research and other types of research such as surveys, individual interviews, and laboratory experiments is that data collection occurs in, and is facilitated by, a group setting. Over the years, much theoretical and empirical research has focused on the behavior of groups and the interactions among people in groups (see Levine & Moreland, 1998, and Snyder & Cantor, 1998, for comprehensive reviews of this literature). This chapter is designed to summarize this knowledge in a way that will place focus group research within a grounded theoretical context and, in turn, aid in the design of valid and more useful focus groups. By understanding the physical, temporal, social, cultural, psychological, and environmental influences on the dynamics of group behavior, we are better able to identify the nature and degree of bias in our analysis and interpretation of focus group data. In general, the usefulness and validity of focus group data are affected by the extent to which participants feel comfortable about openly communicating their ideas, views, or opinions. The wealth of literature on group dynamics suggests that there are many variables that influence participants' "comfort zones." These influences can be grouped into three broad categories: intrapersonal factors and individual differences, interpersonal factors, and environmental factors.

INFLUENCES OF INTRAPERSONAL
FACTORS AND INDIVIDUAL DIFFERENCES

Intrapersonal or individual difference variables include demographic, physical, and personality characteristics. Each individual's unique combination of intrapersonal variables represents a certain behavioral disposition that predisposes the individual to certain modes of behavior in group situations. This behavioral disposition is often "used" by other group members to determine their reactions or responses to a particular individual. These differences in individual characteristics and interpersonal expectations should be carefully considered to maximize focus group participation. For example, in discussing racially sensitive problems, the probability of emotional outbursts in a racially heterogeneous group can be minimized to a certain extent by including persons who are more ethnically homogeneous.

In a group situation, it is important to note the individual characteristics of group members are only part of the picture. In addition, factors that influence group members' interactions with one another relative to one another also determine group behavior and performance. These different interpersonal characteristics influence group cohesiveness, compatibility, and homogeneity/ heterogeneity, which in turn affect group conformity, leadership emergence, bases and uses of power, and interpersonal conflict.

The need to understand individual influences on group processes is underscored by the obvious fact that groups are made up of individuals and that group outcomes are the consequences of individual actions. However, Forsyth (2006) observed that "group members do things to and with each other" (p. 10). As a result, people behave differently when they are in groups than when they are alone. In general, research on diversity suggests that greater heterogeneity is associated with less communication among group members and may even lead to conflict. On the other hand, diversity provides greater perspective and innovation (Levine & Moreland, 1998). In focus group interviewing, the key to success is making the group dynamic work in service of the goals and objectives of the research.

Intrapersonal or individual characteristics influence group processes in two ways. First, the personal characteristics of individuals (e.g., physical, personality, demographic) affect individual behavior in the group and how others react to their words and actions. Second, a particular combination of personal characteristics may influence the group's behavior. For example, an attractive, extraverted person may be perceived to be bright, friendly, and candid and may therefore predispose others in the focus group to respond more favorably to his or her comments or ideas. Focus group participation can then be maximized by increasing interpersonal attraction through appropriate blending or selection of participants. We next consider some of the factors that influence this successful blending.

Demographic Factors

Demographic factors include age, sex, income, occupation, education, religion, and race. The influence of these factors on group dynamics, though pervasive, is often difficult to determine. Further, the relationships that do exist may be difficult to isolate. For example, it is well known that age differences influence group behavior. However, the extent and direction of the influence of age is not well documented. One reason for this may be that the effects of age on group behavior are considered so obvious that controlled studies seem unnecessary. As a result, knowledge of the influence of age on group behavior is based largely on anecdotal evidence (Shaw, 1981). Obviously, some topics are more relevant for some specific age groups than others. It is not age per se that is the critical factor in the composition of such groups.

Age. Age and its effects on the frequency and complexity of interaction have been examined by a number of scholars. Selected findings of studies on age suggest the number and percentage of social contacts increases with age (Beaver, 1932), an individual's ability to empathize increases with age (Dymond, Hughes, & Raabe, 1952), proneness to simultaneous talking and interruptions decrease with age (K. H. Smith, 1977), and risk-taking behavior decreases with age (Chaubey, 1974). There is some evidence to suggest that leadership behavior increases with age, as well (cf. Stogdill's 1948 review of trait studies of leadership). Age may also carry a connotation of status, especially in very diverse groups and in some cultures.

Conformity. Conformity, which is a tendency toward uniformity when individuals interact in a group, also appears to be related to age (cf. Berg & Bass, 1961; Piaget, 1954). Constanzo and Shaw (1966) hypothesized a curvilinear relationship between age and conformity: Conformity increases to a maximum at about age 12 and decreases thereafter. This literature suggests that, other things being equal, a mix of ages may be appropriate for most focus groups. On the other hand, researchers often need to address questions that may require groups that are very homogeneous with respect to age: for example, a study of newly licensed teenage drivers' attitudes regarding safe driving.

Gender. Men and women behave differently in group settings (Deaux & Lafrance, 1998). Sex differences in interpersonal interactions can be attributed to biological factors as well as differences in the social and cultural environments to which they are subjected. Much of this socialization is lifelong and manifested in basic personality differences between men and women. Research on sex differences in personality suggests that men tend to be more aggressive (e.g., physical aggression and nonverbal dominance) than women; women conform more to group pressure than men; women are more sensitive and better able to interpret emotions than men; women are more anxious than men; and men are more confident about their abilities than women (Frieze, 1980; Swim & Campbell, 2003).

These stereotypical sex differences in aggressiveness, dependency, social orientation, and emotionality influence different aspects of interpersonal communication, including nonverbal communication such as body orientation and eye contact. Therefore, the ability to create rapport and maximize the scope and depth of focus group discussion is heavily influenced by the gender composition of the group. This means that care must be exercised when mixing men and women, and the moderator needs to ensure an acceptable level of interaction in mixed-gender groups. This concern may be particularly acute when researching topics that are gender sensitive.

Socioeconomic status. Varying socioeconomic backgrounds of individuals, such as differences in income, occupation, education, and family backgrounds, can affect the dynamics of group interaction. In general, interaction is easier when the group is comprised of individuals with similar socioeconomic backgrounds. Similarity of abilities, intelligence, and knowledge tend to facilitate communication. Similarly, in culturally and racially homogeneous group situations, it may be easier to encourage member participation. This suggests that group members' similarity with respect to socioeconomic status is more likely to maximize interaction within the group. On the other hand, in some situations, researchers may wish to explore directly the dialog and differences among individuals of upper, middle, and lower status.

Physical Characteristics

Physical characteristics of individuals also affect behavior within a group. Characteristics such as size, height, weight, general health, and appearance influence the behavior of others toward the individual, which in turn influences the person's behavior toward the group. For example, Stogdill (1948) found a positive relationship between leadership and weight, height, and measures of the physique. It has been shown that physically attractive persons are rated as more socially skillful and likeable than those less attractive (W. Goldman & Lewis, 1977). Adams and Huston (1975) found that attractive middle-aged adults are judged by both children and adults to be more pleasant, more socially at ease, higher in self-esteem, and of a higher occupational status than less attractive middle-aged adults. The physical characteristics of group members are unlikely to be known to a researcher prior to the actual interview, of course. A skillful interviewer, however, quickly sizes up the group and determines what problems or opportunities are offered by the physical characteristics of the individuals in the group. He or she then adjusts the interview accordingly.

Clothing style affects people's impressions about a person (Gibbins, 1969) and behavior toward him or her (N. Bryant, 1975). However, Shaw (1981) noted that "relative to other variables, these factors are generally weak and can be overcome by effects of more powerful variables such as personality and ability" (p. 186). Yet, there may be some situations when physical appearance may well be the single most important determinant of impressions, such as when impression is based on very limited information or when the initial impression shapes the direction of future interactions (Frieze, 1980). Focus groups, for example, tend to lend themselves to such situations when both observer and participants have to interact with each other based on minimal personal information. Thus, it is probably wise to suggest the manner of dress to group members at the time they are recruited, and the moderator should dress accordingly.

Personality

Personality characteristics interact with demographic variables to influence the behavior of individuals in groups. A personality trait represents a tendency or predisposition to behave in a certain manner across different situations. For example, an aggressive personality is generally expected to display aggressive behavior or tendencies, even in nonthreatening situations. Although the effects of any single personality variable on group behavior may be relatively weak, they can have a significant influence on interpersonal interaction. An aggressive or dominant personality in a focus group situation may, by making emotional and/or negative comments, discourage other participants from being candid with their opinions. Chapter 6 offers suggestions for dealing with such individuals, but it is important for the moderator to quickly size up the personalities of group members and respond accordingly.

The influence of personality characteristics on individual behavior has received a great deal of attention. Shaw (1981) suggested that personality can be represented by relatively few dimensions and these dimensions can be grouped into five broad categories: interpersonal orientation, social sensitivity, ascendant tendencies, dependability, and emotional stability.

Interpersonal orientation refers to the "way or ways an individual views or reacts to other persons" (Shaw, 1981, p. 192). Examples of personality traits that fall under this broad category are approval-orientation, authoritarianism, cyclothymia (approach tendency), and schizothymia (avoidance tendency). *Social sensitivity* can be described as the "degree to which the individual perceives and responds to the needs, emotions, preferences, etc., of the other person" (Shaw 1981, p. 194). It subsumes attributes like empathy, independence, sociability, and social insight, among others. *Ascendant tendencies* refer to the "degree to which individuals assert themselves, and the extent to which they wish to dominate others" (Shaw, 1981, p. 195). It may help explain why certain individuals wish to be prominent in group situations. Examples of ascendant tendencies include assertiveness, dominance, individual prominence, and ascendance.

Interpersonal attraction increases when people can depend on one another. *Dependability* has several dimensions: personal integrity, ability, and behavioral consistency. Interpersonal attraction is increased when people can depend on one another.

> A person who is self-reliant and responsible for his or her actions probably will be viewed as a desirable group member and will contribute to the effectiveness of the group. Similarly, an individual who can be expected to behave in conventional ways is unlikely to disrupt the group, whereas an unconventional person is likely to cause disorder and dissatisfaction. (Shaw, 1981, p. 197)

Finally, *emotional stability* refers to a "class of personality characteristics that are related to the emotional or mental well-being of the individual" (Shaw, 1981, p. 199). These include emotional control, stability, anxiety, defensiveness, neuroticism, and depressive tendencies.

A skillful and experienced focus group moderator will do a quick assessment of these individual characteristics in the first few minutes of the interview and try to make adjustments accordingly. This may involve using a more or less structured approach, depending on which approach will maximize the interaction among all members of the group. We will discuss the efficacy of different approaches and amount of structure for conducting focus groups in Chapter 5.

Additionally, some researchers advocate administering a personality inventory to participants over the telephone prior to their focus group sessions (Quiriconi & Durgan, 1985). By doing this, it is possible to construct homogeneous groups (e.g., only trendsetters or only traditionalists) or heterogeneous personality groups (e.g., both trendsetters and traditionalists), depending on the purpose of the research. Because focus group participants are usually recruited based on demographics and behavior, prior knowledge of the respondents' personalities helps a moderator understand why focus participants are behaving the way they do and how to best interact with them. On the other hand, Krueger and Casey (2000) suggested caution in selecting respondents based on factors like personality, values, and attitudes because these factors can be confounded with other factors that may be important for the research question. For example, selecting respondents who are homogeneous with respect to their attitudes toward a particular social institution, such as public health, may diminish the richness of interaction and dialog among group members regardless of whether the attitudes of group members are primarily positive or primarily negative. Although these numerous studies support some assumptions about the influence of individual differences on a focus group's behavior, unambiguous findings are elusive and confounded by the dynamic interactions among the numerous individual characteristics of group members.

INTERPERSONAL INFLUENCES

Interpersonal interaction is very much affected by expectations about how others will act or behave. These expectations are derived from beliefs about demographic characteristics (e.g., age, sex, and socioeconomic status), personality traits and physical characteristics (e.g., appearance, dress), as well as past experiences. Miller and Turnbull (1986) examined various types of social interaction and concluded that "the expectancy that one person (the perceiver) holds concerning another (the target) affects three phenomena: 1. the target's behavior, 2. the processing of the target's behavior by the perceiver, and 3. the target's perception of him or herself" (p. 234).

Expectations and beliefs are often embodied in stereotypes. The effects of stereotypes on interpersonal processes have received considerable attention (Fiske, 1998; Jones, 1977; Snyder, 1984). Stereotypes tend to be pervasive and resistant to change, and are generally invalid (Ashmore & Del Boca, 1981; Fiske, 1998). Despite the general invalidity of stereotypes, they do influence interpersonal interactions in terms of group cohesiveness, compatibility, and homogeneity/heterogeneity. Furthermore, the perception of social power and its use in enhancing group participation and performance is also influenced by interpersonal expectations. The focus group moderator has an important role in establishing the expectations of the group. He or she must understand that group members bring varying expectations to the group and must subsequently expand these expectations as they meet other members of the group. The moderator needs to take a firm hand and ensure that the expectations of the group members are consistent with and facilitate the purpose of the research.

Group Cohesiveness

Group cohesiveness is what holds a group together. Pennington (2002) defined *cohesiveness* as "the extent to which members of a group are attracted to each other, accept and agree with the priorities and goals of the group and contribute to help achieving the goals" (p. 83). Shaw (1981), however, noted that "at least three different meanings have been attached to the term cohesiveness: (1) attraction to the group, including resistance to leaving it, (2) morale, or the level of motivation evidenced by group members, and (3) coordination of efforts of group members" (p. 213). Although focus groups tend to be temporary, the cohesiveness of a focus group is not a trivial issue. It is important for the group to identify its mission and provide information consistent with this mission if the interview is to be successful. This is something the moderator must facilitate early in the focus group meeting.

The sources of group cohesiveness include most of the variables affecting interpersonal attraction, such as similarity of backgrounds and attitudes. Pennington (2002) listed a variety of factors that influence the cohesiveness of groups, including mutual attraction and similarities with respect to status, goals, and values. This does not mean that focus groups should consist of people who agree perfectly with one another, but it does suggest that groups composed of individuals with violently opposed opinions will be troublesome.

Cohesiveness is also influenced by the degree and nature of communication among group members, proneness to being influenced by other group members, and responsiveness to the actions or feedback from members of the group (Levine & Moreland, 1998). In the context of focus groups, this means that recognition that the group is achieving its purpose can add to the cohesiveness of the group. Occasional comments by the moderator about the quality of the discussion may go a long way toward achieving a sense of cohesiveness and success on the part of the group.

Group cohesiveness influences a number of group processes, such as verbal and nonverbal interaction, the effectiveness of social influence, productivity, and satisfaction of group members. Shaw and Shaw (1962) studied patterns of interaction between groups of children that were high or low in cohesiveness and observed that relative to low-cohesive groups, high-cohesive groups were more cooperative, more friendly, and more praiseworthy of each others' accomplishments. Classic studies by Berkowitz (1954) and Schachter, Ellertson, McBride, and Gregory (1951) suggested that the more cohesive the group, the more power the members have and, therefore, the greater the influence exerted over each other. This means that the cohesiveness of a focus group is a critical element in ensuring interaction. Thus, a sense of cohesiveness may facilitate discussion of even the most sensitive topics.

How strongly attracted members are to the group also affects motivation to work harder to ensure success in the achievement of the group's goals. Van Zelst (1952a, 1952b) found group productivity and cohesiveness to be positively related. These studies also suggest that members belonging to highly cohesive groups experienced greater satisfaction than those in less cohesive groups.

Focus groups are generally considered "fun" by participants. A lively, interesting discussion tends to build a sense of cohesiveness. Equally important, the sharing of experiences and recognition that others have had similar experiences adds to the cohesiveness of the group. It is for this reason that focus group moderators will spend time early in the group discussion seeking common experiences among group members before moving on to more controversial topics.

Group Compatibility, Homogeneity/Heterogeneity

Closely related to group cohesiveness is group *compatibility*, the extent to which members of a group have similar personal characteristics (e.g., needs, personality, attitudes). Compatibility has implications for effective group performance and group satisfaction. In general, highly compatible groups perform their tasks more effectively than less compatible groups because less time and energy are devoted to group maintenance (cf. Haythorn, Couch, Haefner, Langham, & Carter, 1956; Sapolsky, 1960; W. C. Schutz, 1958). Furthermore, compatible groups experience less anxiety and greater satisfaction than incompatible groups (Cohen, 1956; Fry, 1965; Smelser, 1961).

It is important to note that compatibility does not necessarily imply homogeneity, although they are closely related. In evaluating compatibility, emphasis is placed on the relationships among particular characteristics of group members rather than the fact that group member characteristics are homogeneous or heterogeneous (Shaw, 1981). For example, focus group members may be homogeneous in terms of gender but incompatible in terms of socioeconomic status (e.g., income, occupation, social status). On the other hand, focus group members may be homogeneous in terms of gender and compatible in terms of socioeconomic status. Although these two groups are homogeneous in terms of gender, the lack of socioeconomic compatibility in one of the groups may result in different interaction styles and influence the level of group participation. Such differences in the interaction among group members may alter the results obtained from a focus group (cf. Ruhe, 1972; Ruhe & Allen, 1977) and should be taken into account when recruiting respondents and determining the composition of individual groups.

The influence of the composition of a group in terms of gender has been frequently studied by social scientists. This research has consistently found differences in the interaction styles of men and women associated with the gender composition of the group. For example, Aries (1976) found that men are more "personally" oriented, have a greater tendency to address individual members (as opposed to the group as a whole), and speak about themselves more often in mixed-gender groups than in same-sex groups. In all-male groups, men are more concerned with status and competition. By contrast, women in mixed-sex groups tend to be less dominant than in all-female groups. Such research suggests that the nature of the interaction and the quality of the data obtained from a focus group is influenced by the gender composition of the group. It is for this reason that many researchers conduct both same-sex and mixed-gender groups. This practice tends to produce different but complementary insights. It is a practice that also takes maximum advantage of the group as a data collection tool.

Some researchers (cf. Hoffman, 1959; Hoffman & Maier, 1961) believe that heterogeneous groups are generally more effective than homogeneous groups because a variety of skills, perspectives, and knowledge can be brought to bear on the performance of the task. Ruhe (1978) found that mixed-gender groups were more effective than same-sex groups. Closely related to effectiveness in performing group tasks are conformity and the emergence of leadership. There is some evidence to suggest that there is greater conformity among members of mixed-gender groups than among members of same-sex groups because of greater concern about interpersonal relations (Reitan & Shaw, 1964). Thus, the diversity of opinions expressed in a mixed-sex group may be smaller than in a same-sex group.

Dyson, Godwin, and Hazelwood (1976) found that leadership traits are more likely to emerge in mixed-sex groups than in same-sex groups. Leadership behavior generally facilitates objective task accomplishment through the exercise of interpersonal influence and effective communication. This suggests that, topic permitting, mixed-gender groups are more effective in encouraging participation and solving problems than focus groups comprised of members of the same sex. However, if a variety of solutions to problems or responses is desired, it may be better to use same-sex focus groups to reduce the tendency toward conformity common in mixed-gender groups. Ultimately, whether a mixed-gender group or same-sex group is best depends on the nature of the topic. It is important to remember, however, that these two types of groups can produce very different group dynamics and types of information. In general, mixed-gender groups are easier to control for the moderator, but this control may come at the cost of less spontaneity. Less obvious to the focus group researcher is the influence of social power (whether perceived or exercised) on group dynamics, to which we now turn our attention.

Social Power

Social power is the potential or ability to influence others in a group setting (Emerson, 1964). It is an ever present phenomenon that has important implications for small-group interaction and performance. An understanding of the nature of social power and how it can be used to advantage in the context of focus group interviewing is an important component of planning and conducting focus group research.

The ability to influence others in a social situation has traditionally been held to derive from five sources: reward power, coercive power, legitimate power, referent power, and expert power (French & Raven, 1959). In most situations, however, it is the perception of power and not the actual possession of it that influences the behavior of individuals and the reactions of other persons. In the focus group situation, for example, the moderator may be perceived to have more power by virtue of his or her position and ability to dictate the flow and intensity of the discussion. However, certain participants may be perceived to have expert power due to their education, training, and general experience. This expert power may be real or simply perceived. Both types of "experts" pose problems for the focus group moderator, but each must be dealt with differently. In Chapter 6, we discuss specific strategies for dealing with such experts.

Sometimes seating preferences among certain group members may be an indication of their desire to influence the discussion and the opinions of other participants (cf. Hare & Bales, 1963). Behavioral implications of spatial arrangements are discussed in the section of this chapter that considers environmental influences and again in Chapter 6 when we take up the issue of seating participants.

A number of studies suggest that group members who are perceived to possess greater power are better liked than those with less power (Hurwitz, Zander, & Hymovitch, 1953; Lippitt, Polansky, Redl, & Rosen, 1952). This phenomenon appears to be due in part to the fact that a person who possesses power is viewed as the source of rewards and punishment. Further, if a high-power person is liked, he or she is more likely to dispense rewards than punishment. At the same time, a high-power group member is likely to find the group more attractive than a low-power member (Lippitt, Polansky, Redl, & Rosen, 1952; Watson & Bromberg, 1965; Zander & Cohen, 1955). Shaw (1981) noted that "a group member who is highly accepted by the group, who is the target of deferential treatment from others, who has great influence on the group process undoubtedly finds the group more attractive than a member who is not treated so favorably" (p. 313). Thus, the focus group moderator must recognize that certain members of the group may be accorded higher status or power than others within the group. The moderator needs to use this to advantage when it occurs. We discuss strategies for doing so in Chapter 6.

Another factor associated with social power that has implications for focus group interaction is the relationship between power and status. In general, low-status persons are accorded less power and therefore have less influence on the group. Studies of Air Force crew members (Torrance, 1954) support this observation; and it is interesting to note that in these studies, even when the lowest-ranked crew member had the correct solution to a problem, he had little influence on group decision making. Furthermore, Maier and Hoffman (1961) found that a great deal more time and energy is spent in supporting or rejecting the ideas of a high-status person than in finding alternative solutions to a problem. The focus group moderator must be aware of such tendencies and encourage individual idea generation, especially if a variety of perspectives is desired. Further, the moderator needs to legitimize the expression of opinions by lower-status individuals by explicitly asking for such opinions and by providing verbal rewards for such expression. This not only encourages lower status members to speak but also models behavior for the rest of the group that encourages active participation and acceptance of opinions.

Group Participation and Nonverbal Communication

In recent years, the structural (the who and how much of it) and temporal (the when of it) patterns of participation among group members have received increasing interest and greater research attention fueled by the availability of more sophisticated methods for recording, processing, and analyzing information (Hollingshead, 2003; Levine & Moreland, 1998). Researchers are now able to examine a number of issues, such as patterns of interpersonal trust, cognitive load in interactions, self-monitoring in interactions, and patterns of dominance and influence, that have been difficult to examine in detail in the past (cf. McGrath & Kravitz, 1982; Napier & Gershenfeld, 2003).

Of particular interest in the context of focus groups is research on the nonverbal aspects of group interaction. Considerable research exists on gazing and eye contact. Eye contact serves some important functions within the group. McGrath and Kravitz (1982) described its three primary functions within the interpersonal interaction situation: (a) to express interpersonal attitudes such as friendship, agreement, or liking; (b) to collect information about other persons, such as how they are responding to a particular point of view; and (c) to "regulate-synchronize" dyadic conversations (Allen & Guy, 1977; Beattie, 1978; Cary, 1978; Ellsworth, Friedman, Perlick, & Hoyt, 1978; Kendon, 1978; Rutter & Stephenson, 1979; Rutter, Stephenson, Ayling, & White, 1978).

Other nonverbal cues such as smiles (Brunner, 1979; Kraut & Johnston, 1979) and body posture (Bull & Brown, 1977) can also provide useful information during interpersonal interaction. Interpersonal distance or proximity of individuals and its implications for group interaction has also received some research attention and is discussed in the following section.

With respect to the accuracy and effectiveness of nonverbal communication, it has been found that nonverbal decoding accuracy is affected by the sex and the decoding skills of the receiver (Hall, 1978, 1980). Furthermore, when cues in different modes (e.g., audio vs. visual) are contradictory, then receivers are apparently more influenced by visual than by auditory cues (DePaulo, Rosenthal, Eisentat, Rogers, & Finkelstein, 1978). In general, visual cues are often used to compensate or overcome audio difficulties (Krauss, Garlock,

Bricker, & McMahon, 1977). The importance of nonverbal cues in focus group discussions has important implications for the selection and training of moderators, as well as the conduct of a focus group interview. Further, the information represented by nonverbal responses of focus group participants can be useful and complement the information provided via verbal channels of communication. It is for this reason that direct observation or videotaping may be desirable in many focus group research situations. We return to these issues in Chapters 6 and 7.

ENVIRONMENTAL INFLUENCES

The general pleasantness of the focus group environment influences the level of rapport and participation. Studies on spatial arrangements and interpersonal distance, for example, suggest that the seating arrangement and general proximity of participants can affect the ability of participants to talk freely and openly about issues of interest. It is important to recognize that focus groups can be structured in terms of both the composition of group members and the physical layout of the group and room to further the goals of the researcher. Failure to attend to these factors can result in a less than optimal outcome of a focus group exercise.

The purpose of this section is to briefly review some of the more frequently studied aspects of the physical environment, such as territoriality, personal space, spatial arrangements, and the patterns of the communication channel, in addition to the more obvious influences of the material environment, such as shape and size of the room, lighting, ventilation, furniture, and color of the walls. A more detailed treatment of the physical environment determinants of individual and group behavior can be found in Shaw (1981) and Levine and Moreland (1998). These factors have important implications for the conduct of focus groups, and we discuss these implications in the remainder of this chapter.

The Material Environment

Research on the influence of room size on group interaction has particular implications for focus groups. Lecuyer (1975) found that group interaction on a task was more intense in a small room than in a large room. On the other hand, greater polarization of opinions was observed in a small room. The place of furniture and presence of props has also been found to affect interpersonal interaction. For example, Mehrabian and Diamond (1971) observed that preoccupation with a puzzle poster reduced affiliative behavior, such as the amount of conversation, head nodding, eye contact, and verbal reinforcers. On the other hand, the presence of an interesting sculpture facilitated interaction among some individuals but not all. These findings would suggest that the focus group setting be relatively nondescript. Pictures, artwork, or other wall decorations serve to distract members of the group from the task at hand. Indeed, the physical environment should serve to focus the attention of the group on the topic of discussion. When props are used to facilitate discussion, they should be kept hidden until it is time to discuss them.

Territoriality

Territoriality, which refers to the orientations that individuals adopt toward geographical areas and objects in these areas, has significant implications for small-group interaction. Shaw (1981) noted the following:

> When a group member assumes a proprietary right to a particular object, the smooth functioning of the group depends upon the degree to which other group members respect that person's assumed territorial right. For example, if one member adopts a particular chair as his or her own and another sits in it and refuses to move, intra-group conflict is inevitable. (p. 122)

Generally, in focus groups there is a comfortable distance for participants. Participants who must sit too close to others may feel uncomfortable and tend to protect their territory through actions that are not consistent with the purpose of the group. These actions may include withdrawal from the discussion and a tendency to attend to the moderator rather than the group as a whole.

Spatial Arrangements

Spatial arrangements such as seating arrangements can influence group members' perception of status, the degree of participation, patterns of interaction, and leadership behaviors. In a study of seating preferences, Hare and Bales (1963) found that people who scored high on dominance tended to choose the more central seats in the group. Communication among group members seated across the table from one another is significantly greater than among those in other positions (Steinzor, 1950; Strodbeck & Hook, 1961). This suggests that seating a group in a circle, or at least in a fashion where all group members can easily see one another, facilitates discussion and reduces the tendency for particular members of the group to emerge as dominant or for subgroups to emerge.

Interperson Distance

As we noted above, group interaction is also affected by the preferred interperson distance between group members. Shaw (1981) noted that the traditional concept of personal space (Little, 1965; Sommer, 1959), which suggests that people consider the space immediately around their body as personal and private, ignores many personal, social, and situational variables. For example, interpersonal distances between friends are smaller than between strangers. Even among strangers, interpersonal distances vary according to the individuals' demographic characteristics, such as age, sex, and socioeconomic and cultural backgrounds. Interpersonal distances increase with age through adolescence and sometimes beyond (Baxter, 1970; Tennis & Dabbs, 1975).

The nature of relationships between individuals also affects preferred face-to-face distances (Little, 1965; Meisels & Guardo, 1969). Interperson distances tend to be greater for strangers than for acquaintances and greater for acquaintances than for friends. In general, females tend to prefer closer interperson distances than males (Patterson & Schaeffer, 1977; Willis, 1966). Perceptions of relative social status can influence preferred interperson distances. A study by Lott and Sommer (1967) suggested that interperson distance does not indicate which person has a higher status because people tend to distance themselves from both higher- and lower-status persons.

These studies make it clear that the issues of territoriality and person space are not simple. Rather, the comfortable distance and seating arrangement for a particular focus group depends to some extent on the composition of the group: whether it is mixed gender or same sex, the socioeconomic status of the members of the group, and the cultural or subcultural background of the participants. These issues must be considered during the design phase of focus group research and should be resolved in a manner consistent with the purpose of the research and the need to maximize participation by all members of the group.

Moderated Groupings of Strangers

The wealth of theory and research on group dynamics provides a useful starting point for understanding the dynamics of interaction in a focus group and for identifying factors that may facilitate or impede the research objectives of a focus group. However, the implications of this body of knowledge must be tempered with an understanding of the unique characteristics of focus groups and the realities associated with applying general principles of group dynamics to the management and analysis of focus groups. The temporary nature of focus groups may limit the ability to manage and, more important, predict the influence of certain demographic factors such as age, sex, and occupation on openness of interpersonal communication. Therefore, research findings based on long-term observations of group members in the work or social environment may not always apply to focus group members who in all likelihood are perfect strangers and therefore do not have the time to really develop a rapport. As noted earlier, A. E. Goldman (1962) describes these circumstances as "groupings" rather than groups. Yet, much of the research on group dynamics has been carried out within the context of the same type of group that defines a focus group: temporary groups brought together for a specific purpose that are disbanded once the purpose is served.

A frequent but rarely tested assumption about the focus group interview is that better data are obtained when participants are strangers. For example, Morgan (1998) argued that acquaintances can seriously upset the dynamics of the group and inhibit responses. He also suggested that the need for strangers to explain themselves and their points of view to one another adds to the information value of the group. Friends and acquaintances are more likely to possess tacit knowledge about one another that allows them to communicate without fully articulating assumptions and context.

Fern (1982) tested this acquaintanceship assumption and concluded that an aggregation of the independent responses of individuals who are unknown to one another and who do not meet as a group is just as effective for generating ideas as focus groups. Further, although differences between focus groups and unmoderated groups in terms of quantity and quality of ideas are modest, the differences do favor focus groups. Generally, focus group sessions are preceded by "get-acquainted" and "warm-up" sessions that usually provide participants limited but ample opportunity to get to know one another. Thus, the issue of acquaintanceship appears to be a matter of degree in most focus groups, and its influence appears modest at best.

There are times, of course, when the purpose of a group requires the use of acquaintances, friends, or close relatives. Groups consisting of husbands and wives, parents and children, and coworkers are common and can provide especially useful insights. It is important to recognize, however, that such groups produce rather different information than would be obtained from strangers or even from the same people interviewed in a different context. Thus, separating husbands from wives or parents from children to form two groups most certainly produces different social dynamics and different information.

The casual, voluntary nature of focus group participation may reduce participants' motivation to participate in the group's mission of sharing ideas and responses to problem situations. The temporary nature of focus groups may also affect the efficacy of certain strategies used to influence focus group outcomes. In the work environment, rewards like promotions and bonuses are often used to bring out the best in the individual and the group. On the other hand, the temporary nature of the focus group and the lack of acquaintance among the members may facilitate discussion because there are few consequences associated with each member expressing his or her views. The task for the focus group moderator is to overcome the limitations arising from the temporary nature of the group and use the temporary and unique characteristics of the group to facilitate information sharing.

The moderator must also deal with the consequences of his or her presence. The presence of a moderator or facilitator, who is almost always a stranger to the group, may create an atmosphere of artificiality and potentially inhibit the free flow of discussion. In work-related groups, leaders gradually emerge or are appointed by group members or authorities to provide direction and motivation for the achievement of group goals. The moderator of a focus group is thrust on the group and is entrusted with the sometimes difficult tasks of creating rapport and motivating participants to share their ideas and feelings. Although this "artificial" leader may hinder the group in some ways, this designated leader eliminates much of the distraction associated with the group developing its own pattern of leadership. We have more to say about the role of the moderator in Chapter 5.

Focus groups do share many of the characteristics of other small groups. They are, however, also unique with respect to their purpose, composition, and duration. The unique characteristics of focus groups may appear to be one of the limitations of this type of research, but they also provide potential advantages in certain situations. The limitations may be partially overcome by pre-group screening interviews, providing incentives for participation, selecting a convenient time and place for the meeting, and employing a well-trained moderator. Proactive efforts to overcome the limitations of focus groups and to build on knowledge of small-group dynamics set the stage for exploiting the unique advantages of the group interview and go a long way toward creating an atmosphere conducive to active group participation.

CONCLUSION

The substantial body of literature on group dynamics provides a general foundation on which to build a methodology for the focus group interview. Any particular focus group research project will benefit from prior careful consideration of how individual differences, interpersonal factors, and environmental factors are likely to affect a group's behavioral dynamics. In the next chapter, we consider some of the practical issues associated with ensuring that the groups are designed to maximize the accomplishment of the researchers' purpose.

REVIEW QUESTIONS

1. An adequate understanding of group dynamics is an essential prerequisite for the conduct of any meaningful focus group. Discuss.

2. How can personal characteristics of focus group participants influence the nature and intensity of interaction?

3. How can we use our knowledge of environmental influences such as spatial arrangements and the physical environment to enhance focus group participation?

4. Why must a qualitative researcher be wary of certain sexual or racial stereotypes when conducting focus groups?

5. Discuss some influences of personality on focus group dynamics.

6. Individuals behave differently when in groups than when they are alone. What are some of the group processes (e.g., cohesiveness, leadership emergence) that can affect the productivity of focus groups?

7. Why is it important for the moderator to pay attention to nonverbal aspects of group participation?

8. Under what conditions would a qualitative researcher prefer more heterogeneity among focus group participants?

9. Acknowledging the fact that gender differences in attitudes seem inevitable, what are some basic behavioral considerations in designing a focus group study to understand contraceptive usage among men and women?

10. When is physical appearance an important determinant of group interaction? How does the physical appearance of a moderator affect his or her ability to conduct focus groups effectively?

Exercise: Find a place, such as a library, restaurant, or coffee shop, and observe the behavior of several groups. Note who the group members are, who appears dominant, and how strongly each member is affiliated with the group. You should be able to make these determinations by observation from a distance. What cues give you information about the group? How would such cues be useful to a focus group moderator?

3

Focus Groups and the Research Toolbox

In the time since Merton's pioneering work, focus groups have become an important research tool for applied social scientists who work in program evaluation, marketing, public policy, the health sciences, advertising, and communications. Focus group interviews are but one type of group research, however, though many of these group techniques have significant communalities. Other group research techniques are discussed in Chapter 9. This chapter provides an overview of the basic elements and issues involved in focus group research.

FOCUS GROUP BASICS: STRUCTURE, PROCESS, AND DATA

A. E. Goldman (1962) differentiated group depth interviews from other techniques by examining the meaning of the three words in the name. A *group* is "a number of interacting individuals having a community of interest" (p. 61); *depth* involves "seeking information that is more profound than is usually accessible at the level of interpersonal relationships" (p. 63); and *interview* implies the presence of a moderator who "uses the group as a device for eliciting information" (p. 64). The term *focus* in the full title simply implies that the interview is limited to a small number of issues. The importance of the group as a means for eliciting information has been emphasized by G. H. Smith (1954) in his classic definition of group interviewing: "The term *group interviewing* will be limited to those situations when the assembled group is small enough to permit genuine discussion among all its members" (p. 59).

The contemporary focus group interview generally involves 8 to 12 individuals who discuss a particular topic under the direction of a moderator who promotes interaction and ensures that the discussion remains on the topic of interest. Experience has shown that smaller groups may be dominated by one or two members and that larger groups are difficult to manage and inhibit participation by all members of the group. A typical focus group session will last from 1.5 to 2.5 hours. Although they can be conducted in a variety of sites ranging from homes to offices and by conference telephone, it is most common for focus groups to be held in facilities designed especially for focus group interviewing. Such facilities provide one-way mirrors and viewing rooms where observers may unobtrusively watch the interview in progress.

Focus group facilities may also include equipment for audio- or videotaping the interview and perhaps even a small transmitter for the moderator to wear (a "bug-in-the-ear") so that observers may have input into the interview. Such facilities tend to be situated in locations that are either easy to get to, such as just off a major commuter traffic artery, or in places like shopping malls where people tend naturally to gather. Over 1,000 such facilities exist in the United States today.

The moderator is the key to ensuring that the group discussion goes smoothly. The focus group moderator is generally (but not always) well trained in group dynamics and interview skills. Depending on the intent of the research, the moderator may be more or less directive with respect to the discussion and often is quite nondirective, letting the discussion flow naturally as long as it remains on the topic of interest. Indeed, one of the strengths of focus group research is that it may be adapted to provide the most desirable level of focus and structure. If researchers are interested in how parents have adapted to the child care requirements created by dual careers, the interviewer can ask very general and nonspecific questions about the topic in order to determine the most salient issues on the minds of the participants. On the other hand, if the interest of the researchers is parents' reactions to alternative concepts for child care, the interviewer can provide detailed information about the concepts and ask very specific questions about each one.

The moderator might also be more or less directive in this example by drilling down from an initial series of general questions about child care, then moving the discussion to more specific issues as the group proceeds. In fact, it is quite common for an interviewer to start a group with some general questions and then switch the focus of the group to more specific issues as the discussion progresses.

It is important to recognize that the amount of direction provided by the interviewer does influence the types and quality of the data obtained from the group. The interviewer provides the agenda or structure for the discussion by virtue of his or her leadership role in the group. When a moderator suggests a new topic for discussion by asking a new question, the group has a tendency to comply. A group discussion might never cover particular topics or issues unless the moderator intervenes to move things forward. This raises the question of the most appropriate amount of structure for a given group. There is, of course, no best answer to this question because the amount of structure and the directness of the moderator must be determined by the broader research agenda that gave rise to the focus groups: the types of information sought, the specificity of the information required, and the way the information will be used.

There is also a balance that must be struck between what is important to members of the group and what is important to the researchers. Less structured groups will tend to pursue those issues and topics of greater importance, relevance, and interest to the group. This is perfectly appropriate if the objective of the researcher is to learn about those things that are most important to the group. Often, however, the researcher has rather specific information needs. Discussion of issues relevant to these information needs may only occur when the moderator takes a more directive and structured approach. It is important to remember that when this occurs, participants are discussing what is important to the researcher, not necessarily what they consider significant.

Although focus group research can produce quantitative data, focus groups are almost always carried out with the collection of qualitative data as their primary purpose. This is their advantage, because focus groups produce a very rich body of data expressed in the respondents' own words and context. There is a minimum of artificiality of response, unlike survey questionnaires that ask for responses expressed on 5-point rating scales or other constrained response categories. Participants can qualify their responses or identify important contingencies associated with their answers. Thus, responses have a certain ecological validity not found in traditional survey research. This often makes the data provided by focus groups idiosyncratic, however. It also makes the results of focus group research more difficult and challenging to summarize and generalize. This does not mean that quantitative tools cannot be applied to the analysis and interpretation of focus group data, however. Quantitative methods can be used to analyze focus group data, and we will discuss how this might be done in Chapter 7. Also, quantitative data (e.g., simple surveys) can be gathered in focus groups to anchor respondents' viewpoints as a basis for further dialogue and elaboration.

Focus group research has been the subject of much controversy and criticism. Such criticism is generally associated with two concerns: first, the view that focus group interviews do not yield "hard" quantitative data and, second, the concern that group members may not be representative of a larger population, because both the small sample numbers and the idiosyncratic nature of the group discussion. Such criticism is unfair, however. Although focus groups do have important limitations of which the researcher should be aware, these limitations are not unique to focus group research, and they are not "fatal flaws," as all research tools in the social sciences have significant limitations.

The key to successfully using focus groups in social science research is ensuring that their use is consistent with the objectives and purpose of the research. Indeed, this is also true of the successful use of all social science research methods. Focus groups may serve a variety of purposes, depending on where in the research agenda they are applied and how. For example, focus groups are often a useful starting point for the design of survey questionnaires because they provide a means for exploring the way potential respondents talk about objects and events, identifying alternatives for closed-ended survey items, and determining the suitability of various types of scaling approaches. Although they are most often used for such exploratory research, they do have a place as confirmatory tools. For example, the responses of the members of one or two focus groups who are representative of a larger population may be sufficient to determine whether the humor used in an advertising execution is on the mark or lost on the respondents. Focus groups are also sometimes used later in a particular research process. For example, when quantitative marketing research of a set of new product concepts yields inconclusive (tie) results, focus groups can often tease out the subtler sources of a concept's appeal or lack of it.

If focus groups can be used for both exploration and confirmation, the question arises of how focus groups differ from other tools of science and what purpose(s) they serve that are not served by other methods. The answer lies in the nature or character of the data generated by focus group interviews. Krippendorf (2004) distinguishes between two types of data: emic and etic. *Emic data* are data that arise in a natural or indigenous form. They are only minimally imposed by the researcher or the research setting. *Etic data,* on the other hand, represent the researcher's imposed view of the situation. Little of the research that is actually carried out can be described as completely etic or completely emic. Even the most structured type of research will be influenced to some extent by the idiosyncratic nature of the respondent and his or her environment. On the other hand, even the most natural of situations may not yield data that are completely emic because the researcher must make decisions about what to attend to and what to ignore. Thus, it is perhaps more useful to think of a continuum of research, with some methods lying closer to the emic end of the continuum and some techniques lying closer to the etic end.

Focus groups, along with other techniques like unstructured individual depth interviews, projective methods, and ethnographies, provide data that are closer to the emic end of the continuum because they allow individuals to respond in their own words using their own categorizations and perceived associations. They are not completely void of structure, however, because the researcher does raise questions of one type or another. Survey research and experimentation tend to produce data that are closer to the etic end of the continuum because the response categories used by the respondent have been generally prescribed by the researcher. These response categories may or may not be those with which the respondent is comfortable, though the respondent may still select an answer. And, even when closed-ended survey questions are the only options available, some respondents elect to give answers in their own words, as most experienced survey researchers have discovered.

Neither emic nor etic data are better or worse than the other; they simply differ. Each has its place in social science research; each complements the other. Each serves to compensate for the limitations of the other. Indeed, one way to view social science research is as a process that moves from the emic to the etic and back in a cycle. Phenomena that are not well understood are often first studied with tools that yield more emic data. As a particular phenomenon is better understood and greater theoretical and empirical structure is built around it, tools that yield more etic types of data tend to predominate. As knowledge accumulates, it often becomes apparent that the explanatory structure surrounding a given phenomenon is incomplete. This frequently leads to the need for data that are more emic, and the process continues.

The philosophical issues associated with this view are beyond the scope of this book. The interested reader can find further discussion of these issues in Bliss, Monk, and Ogborn (1983) and Bogdan and Biklen (1982). Nevertheless, an understanding of emic versus etic provides a useful way of distinguishing the purpose and value of focus group interviewing.

USES OF FOCUS GROUPS: APPLICATIONS, ADVANTAGES, AND LIMITATIONS

Focus groups may be useful at virtually any point in a research program, but they are particularly useful for exploratory research when rather little is known about the phenomenon of interest. As a result, focus groups tend to be used very early in a research project and are often followed by other types of research that provide more precise quantitative data from larger samples of respondents. As mentioned earlier, focus groups have also been proven useful following the analysis of a large-scale quantitative survey. In this latter use, the focus group facilitates interpretation of quantitative results and adds depth to the responses obtained in the more structured survey. Focus groups also have a place as a confirmatory method that may be used for testing hypotheses. This latter application may arise when the researcher has strong reasons to believe a hypothesis is correct and when confirmation by even a small group would tend to result in rejection of the hypothesis.

A variety of research needs lend themselves to the use of focus group interviews. Bellenger and colleagues (1976) and Higgenbotham and Cox (1979) provide detailed discussions and examples of the use of focus groups, particularly in a marketing application context. Among the more common uses of focus groups are the following:

1. Obtaining general background information about a topic of interest
2. Generating research hypotheses that can be submitted to further research and testing using more quantitative approaches

3. Stimulating new ideas and creative concepts

4. Diagnosing the potential for problems with a new program, service, or product

5. Generating impressions of products, programs, services, institutions, or other objects of interest

6. Learning how respondents talk about the phenomenon of interest. This, in turn, may facilitate the design of questionnaires, survey instruments, or other research tools that might be employed in more quantitative research.

7. Interpreting previously obtained quantitative results

This list illustrates the impressive breadth of application of focus group research, but it is hardly exhaustive. One of the most appealing features of focus groups is their robust versatility for shedding light on almost any topic or issue. Focus groups are also widely used because they provide useful information and offer the researcher a number of advantages. This information and the advantages of the technique come at a price, however. We briefly discuss the relative advantages and disadvantages of focus groups and then turn to a discussion of the steps involved in the use and design of focus groups.

Advantages of Focus Groups

Focus groups provide a number of advantages relative to other types of research:

1. Focus groups provide data from a group of people much more quickly and often at less cost than would be the case if each individual were interviewed separately. They can also be assembled on much shorter notice than would be required for a more systematic and larger survey. In marketing studies, focus group data analysis often begins immediately after a session ends, yielding preliminary findings quickly.

2. Focus groups allow the researcher to interact directly with respondents. This provides opportunities for the clarification of responses, for follow-up questions, and for the probing of responses. Respondents can qualify responses or give contingent answers to questions. In addition, it is possible for the researcher to observe nonverbal responses such as gestures, smiles, frowns, and so forth, which may carry information that supplements and on occasion even contradicts the verbal response.

3. The open response format of a focus group provides an opportunity to obtain large and rich amounts of data in the respondents' own words. The researcher can obtain deeper levels of meaning, make important connections, and identify subtle nuances in expression and meaning.

4. Focus groups allow respondents to react to and build on the responses of other group members. This synergistic effect of the group setting may result in the production of data or ideas that might not have been uncovered in individual interviews. Differences of opinion among group members also help researchers identify how and why individuals embrace or reject particular ideas, communications, or products.

5. Focus groups are very flexible. They can be used to examine a wide range of topics with a variety of individuals and in a variety of settings.

6. Focus groups may be one of the few research tools available for obtaining data from children or from individuals who are not particularly literate.

7. The results of a focus group are extremely user friendly and easy to understand. Researchers and decision makers can readily understand the verbal responses of most respondents. This is not always the case with more sophisticated survey research that employs complex statistical analyses.

Limitations of Focus Groups

Although focus groups are valuable research tools and offer a number of advantages, they are not a panacea for all research needs, and they do have their limitations. Many of these limitations are simply the negative side of the advantages listed above:

1. The small numbers of respondents that participate in even several different focus groups and the convenience nature of most focus group recruiting practices significantly limit generalization to a larger population. Indeed, persons who are willing to travel to a locale to participate in a 1- to 2-hour group discussion may be quite different from the population of interest, at least on some dimension such as compliance or deference.

2. The interaction of respondents with one another and with the moderator may have two undesirable effects. First, the responses from members of the group are not independent of one another, which restricts the generalizability of results. Second, the results obtained in a focus group may be biased by a very dominant or opinionated member. More reserved group members may be hesitant to talk.

3. The "live" and immediate nature of the interaction may lead a researcher or decision maker to place greater faith in the findings than is actually warranted. There is a certain credibility attached to the opinions of live and present respondents that is often not present in statistical summaries.

4. The open-ended nature of responses obtained in focus groups often makes summarization and interpretation of results difficult.

5. The moderator may bias results by knowingly or unknowingly providing cues about what types of responses and answers are desirable or seeking to achieve group consensus on particular topics.

Thus, we see that focus groups offer important advantages, but these same advantages have associated dangers and limitations.

As we noted above, focus groups are most often used as a preliminary stage in a research program that eventually includes a larger, more representative survey of the population or as a means for adding insight to the results obtained from a survey. We should not overlook the cases in which focus groups alone may be a sufficient basis for decision making, however. One example of such a case in an applied research setting would be the identification of flaw in a program or a serious problem with a new product that would necessitate redesign. Another would be a situation in which there is reason to believe that the group of people, or population, of interest is relatively homogeneous, at least with respect to the issue at hand. In such cases, a small number of respondents is all that is needed to generalize to the larger population. Reynolds and Johnson (1978) provide a useful example of the complementary use of focus groups and survey research.

It is true that focus groups yield qualitative data obtained from relatively small numbers of respondents who interact with one another, yet this is exactly their purpose. There are those who would use focus groups to explore all manner of research questions, though the issue could more appropriately be addressed by a survey or an experiment. This view is as inappropriate as the view that dismisses the focus group as having no utility. The focus group is one tool in the social scientist's research tool kit. It should be used when it is appropriate and for the purposes for which it was designed. Other tools should be used for other purposes. It has been said that to a man with a hammer, everything is a nail. There is an unfortunate tendency among some social scientists to view the world in the same way. Thus, they tend to regard focus groups as appropriate or inappropriate, sound or unsound, without regard to the research question. Focus groups are appropriate—more appropriate than more quantitative techniques—for certain classes of problems. Other tools are more appropriate for other classes of problems.

Focus groups have a long history as an important tool for discovery and exploration. When little is known about a particular subject or a certain phenomenon, there are few research alternatives. Some type of orienting, human interview will be required. The options available are individual interviews or focus groups. Focus groups provide a more rapid and often cost-efficient means for completing interviews. On the other hand, focus groups are not always inexpensive because respondent recruiting and compensation costs vary considerably according to the characteristics of the sample. For example, it is easier to find and cheaper to compensate a sample of individuals who eat potato chips than one comprised of neurosurgeons. Also, the view that focus groups are less expensive than other viable research alternatives often fails to take into account significant travel, food, and other costs associated with focus group road trips. Table 3.1 lists a number of other advantages of focus groups relative to individual interviews. The decision to use focus groups instead of individual interviews must recognize the potential for confounding of individual responses, however.

STEPS IN THE DESIGN AND USE OF FOCUS GROUPS

Research employing focus groups shares many of the same characteristics and procedures as other types of research. Figure 3.1 lists the sequence of steps in the design and use of focus groups. Like all research, focus group research must begin with a problem. Focus groups are designed to do exactly what the name implies: focus. A focus group is not a freewheeling conversation among group members; it has focus and a clearly identifiable agenda. Problem definition requires a clear statement of what kinds of information are desirable and from whom this information should be obtained. A clear understanding of the problem or general research question is critical because it gives rise to the specific questions that should be raised by the moderator and identifies the population of interest.

Once a clear statement of the problem has been generated, it is possible to move to the second stage of the research. Like any survey, it is important to identify a sampling frame. A sampling frame is a list of people (households, organizations) that the researcher has reason to believe is representative of the larger population of interest. The sampling frame is the operational definition of the population. The identification of a sound sampling frame is far more critical in large-scale survey research than it is for focus group research, however. Because it is inappropriate to generalize far beyond the members of focus groups, the sampling frame need only be a good approximation of the population of interest. Thus, if the research were concerned with middle-class parents of school children, a membership list for the local PTA might be an appropriate sampling frame.

The definition of the research question and identification of the sampling frame provide important information for the third step in the focus group design process: identification of a moderator and design of the interview guide. Both the moderator and the types and forms of questions included in the interview guide should be compatible with the group to be interviewed.

TABLE 3.1
Advantages of Focus Groups Relative to Individual Interviews

Respondent Interaction Advantages

1. *Synergism.* The combined effort of the group will produce a wider range of information, insight, and ideas than will the cumulation of the responses of a number of individuals when these replies are secured privately. (But note, some researchers suggest that this is not always the case.)

2. *Snowballing.* A bandwagon effect often operates in a group interview situation, in that a comment by one individual often triggers a chain of responses from the other participants.

3. *Stimulation.* Usually after a brief introductory period, the respondents get "turned on," in that they want to express their ideas and expose their feelings as the general level of excitement over the topic increases in the group.

4. *Security.* In an interviewer-interviewee situation, respondents may not be willing to expose their views for fear of having to defend these views or of appearing "unconcerned," "radical," or whatever the case may be. In the well-structured group, on the other hand, "the individual can usually find some comfort in the fact that his feelings are not greatly different from those of his peers, and that he or she can expose an idea without necessarily being forced to defend, follow through or elaborate on it. He or she is more likely to be candid because the focus is on the group rather than the individual; the respondent soon realizes that the things he or she says are not necessarily being identified with him or her" (Hess, 1968, p. 194).

5. *Spontaneity.* Because no individual is required to answer any given question in a group interview, the individual's responses can be more spontaneous and less conventional, and should provide a more accurate picture of the person's position on some issue. In the group interview, people speak only when they have definite feelings about a subject and not because a question requires a response.

Sponsor Advantages

1. *Serendipity.* It is more often the case in a group, rather than an individual interview, that some idea will "drop out of the blue." The group also affords the opportunity to develop it to its full significance.

2. *Specialization.* The group interview allows the use of a more highly trained but more expensive interviewer because a number of individuals are being "interviewed" simultaneously.

3. *Scientific scrutiny.* The group interview allows closer scrutiny. First, the session itself can be observed by several others. This affords some check on the consistency of the interpretations. Second, the session may be tape recorded or even videotaped. Later, detailed examination of the recorded session allows additional insight and also can help clear up points of disagreement among analysts.

4. *Structure.* The group interview affords more control than the individual interview with regard to the topics that are covered and the depth with which they are treated because the "interviewer" in the role of moderator has the opportunity to reopen topics that received too shallow a discussion when initially presented.

5. *Speed.* Because a number of individuals are being interviewed at the same time, the group interview permits the securing of a given number of interviews more quickly than do individual interviews.

SOURCE: Hess (1968).

The moderator who is well suited for interviewing children may be inappropriate as a moderator of a group of design engineers who will be discussing the technical characteristics of a complex product. Questions that might be used with computer programmers and systems analysts would probably be worded differently from those used with the lay user of personal computers.

It is common for the identification of the moderator and design of the interview guide to be carried out simultaneously with the recruitment of participants for the focus groups. The recruitment process requires identification of a time and place for the group. Special facilities or equipment that might be required to carry out portions of the interview may dictate a special type of setting, which must be identified in reasonable proximity to potential participants. Persons in the sampling frame are contacted and asked to participate in a group at a particular time and place. They are usually informed of the general topic for the interview because this often stimulates interest and increases the probability of participation. It is also usually customary to offer participants an incentive for participation. Depending on the research budget and the type of participants recruited, incentives range from small gifts to several hundred dollars per person.

It is generally best to recruit a few more participants than the number desired. Participants often cancel at the last minute, get stuck in traffic, have unexpected

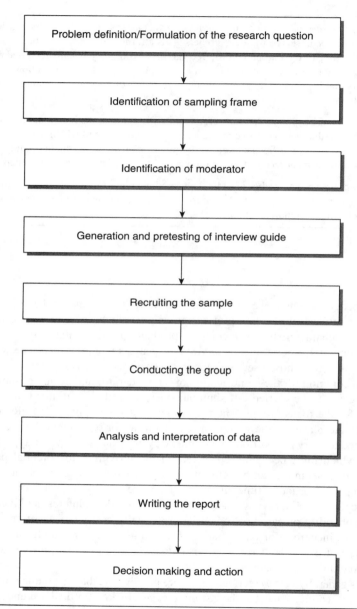

Figure 3.1   Steps in the Design and Use of Focus Groups

emergencies, or otherwise fail to arrive at the designated time and place. After recruiting the participants, it is generally a good idea to follow up with a reminder by telephone or mail a day or two before the group is scheduled.

The focus group interview itself is the next step in the process. The moderator leads the group through the questions on the interview guide and seeks to facilitate discussion among all the group members. This discussion may be audio- or videotaped to facilitate later analysis. The last phases of focus group research are also similar to those in other types of research. These latter two phases are analysis and interpretation of data and report writing.

Each of the phases outlined above will be discussed in greater detail in later chapters.

CONCLUSION

Focus group research is a useful research tool, but there are many other tools in the toolbox. It is important to recognize the unique strengths and limitations of focus group research. Focus group research produces very specific types of data that are at once very rich and diagnostic and limited. The use of focus groups can produce powerful insights, but such use is not a substitute for other research techniques.

REVIEW QUESTIONS

1. What are the key characteristics of a focus group?

2. What are the differences between emic and etic categorization? How do these differences relate to the use of focus groups?

3. What are the primary uses of focus groups? When would it be appropriate to use a focus group instead of a set of individual interviews? A standardized survey?

4. What are the advantages and disadvantages of focus groups relative to surveys? Relative to controlled experiments?

5. Why is it important to have a clear definition of the research question(s) prior to initiating a focus group?

6. What does it mean to say that a good focus group is not too unstructured and not too structured? What provides the structure of the agenda for a focus group?

7. What does it mean to say that the results of a focus group are only as good as the moderator? Why is this so?

8. How are the results of focus groups interpreted? Why is interpretation sometimes difficult?

9. What actions or decisions might be appropriate based on the results obtained from a focus group?

10. Why is it often useful to do several focus groups on the same topic?

11. What alternatives are available to the researcher when it is not possible to bring people together as a group or when the interaction of group members may be undesirable?

Exercise: Think of a topic with which you are familiar but that involves some degree of controversy (e.g., abortion or aid to AIDS victims). Design several survey-type questions with specific closed-ended responses. Convene a small group (these may be just a few friends). Ask your questions without offering the alternatives you have generated. Near the end, offer your alternatives to the group and ask how well they capture the opinions of the group's members. Compare the responses of the group's members with your original survey items. What do you learn about the use of group interviews? About closed-ended survey questions?

4

Recruiting Focus Group Participants and Designing the Interview Guide

Focus groups are conducted to obtain specific types of information from a clearly identified set of individuals. This means that individuals who are invited to participate in a focus group must be both able and willing to provide the desired information and must be representative of the population of interest. Thus the selection and recruitment of participants for a focus group is a critical task. So too is the design of the interview guide because it establishes the agenda for the group discussion and provides a structure within which participants may interact and articulate their thoughts and feelings. A focus group is not just a haphazard discussion or brainstorming among people who happen to be available; it is a well-planned research endeavor that requires the same care and attention that is associated with any other type of scientific research.

Two critical elements in successful focus group research are the recruitment of participants and the design of the interview guide. The interview guide establishes the agenda for the discussion of the group. The nature of the discussion is determined in large measure by the composition of the group and the interaction that ensues among its members. Thus the interview guide and the selection of group members may be viewed, in one sense, as the construction of the research instrument.

The review of group dynamics in Chapter 2 suggests that particular care must be given to the composition of the group because the quality of the discussion and perhaps even its direction may be determined by the interaction of the particular set of people who are brought together. For example, if a group of technical specialists is brought together to discuss a complex problem, it is likely that the discussion will take on a very different character than if the group were composed of a few technical people, a few nontechnical but knowledgeable lay persons, and a few novices. A group composed of parents and children will produce a very different type of discussion than a group composed of parents or children alone. Mixed-gender groups often give rise to different outcomes and group dynamics than do single-sex groups.

The relative homogeneity of groups, on a variety of characteristics, may also influence the dynamics of the group. Such differences are not a cause for dismay. They simply suggest that when a group is a part of the measurement tool, considerable care must be exercised in its design and composition. The researcher should consider the impact of group composition early in the design phase of the project and ensure that membership in any given focus group is consistent with the objectives of the research. This means that the research agenda and its objectives must be established clearly and very early. Too often focus group participants are recruited based on only a few demographic or behavioral characteristics and with little sensitivity to more subtle but equally important aspects of group compositions.

In this chapter, we consider the construction of the focus group as a research instrument. We consider both the recruiting process and the construction of the interview guide. Both activities must be guided by the purpose of the research. Thus we begin our discussion with consideration of the research agenda.

ESTABLISHING THE RESEARCH AGENDA

Focus group research does not differ from other forms of research where problem formulation and the specification of research objectives are concerned. Although focus groups are frequently used and are particularly helpful when little is known about a phenomenon, this does not mean that a focus group should be a substitute for problem formulation. Focus groups are not designed to be opportunities for a group of people to discuss whatever comes to mind; they are designed with a particular purpose in mind. Too often focus groups are used as a substitute for thinking about a topic with the result being that very little useful information is obtained from the group. There is a considerable difference between not knowing very much about a particular phenomenon and not knowing what you want to learn.

The first step in establishing the research agenda is problem formulation. *Problem formulation* is simply the specification of what problem is being addressed, what information is sought, and for what purpose. Indeed, it will not be clear that a focus group is the most appropriate type of research for the question at hand until the problem has been clearly defined. For example, a research question involving the evaluation of the effects of a specific television commercial would be better answered with an experimental design than a focus group. This question requires a quantitative answer to the question of "how much" of an effect the commercial has on some standard measure. On the other hand, a research question focused on the identification of specific problems consumers encounter in obtaining service at the local office of the department of motor vehicles would be a good match with focus group research. In this latter case, the need is for discovery and for answers related to the question of "what kinds" of problems.

An old adage holds that "A problem well defined is half solved." This is as true for focus group research as it is for any other type of research. Only by careful definition of the research question can the type of group required be identified. As we will see, the definition of the research problem is also critical to the design of the interview guide. Consider the general research question of consumers' views regarding the presence of violence in video games. As stated, this question is not sufficiently focused because it does not indicate which consumers (parents, teenagers, users, or some other group) or what views (the entertainment value of the games, the perceived harmful effects, or some other effect). Although the views of all of these groups of consumers on all of these topics may ultimately be of interest, any one focus group or small number of multiple groups will be able to address only a limited number of respondents and a limited number of topics. A very general research question will produce very general and not very useful results.

Problem formulation must begin with an assessment of what is already known about the phenomenon of interest and what additional information is required. The purpose of research may be to inform a decision, identify alternative hypotheses or courses of action, confirm a hypothesis, explore a defined domain of behavior, or provide the solution to any of hundreds of other large and small problems. The purpose of the research must be clearly identified in terms of desired outcomes and the information to be obtained related specifically to these outcomes. This is a thought process in which the researcher and all parties with a stake in the research should participate.

A well-defined research question is one that clearly identifies the topic of the research, the population that is relevant to the question, and the specific issues of interest. Thus, in the case of the video game example above, the research question might be stated as the views regarding the entertainment value of violence among adolescent males who regularly play computer games. Of course, another different but equally valid research question might be stated in terms of the concerns regarding the usefulness of labels regarding violence in video games among parents of teenage males. Although both the former and latter questions are quite valid and potentially useful, they lead to very different types of groups and very different types of questions. Defining a research question too broadly or at too general a level is likely to produce an unsatisfactory outcome. Focus group research is a tool for exploring a topic in detail. Once the research question has been clearly articulated, it is possible to move on to the recruitment of subjects and the design of an interview guide.

RECRUITING PARTICIPANTS

Participants in focus groups can be recruited in a variety of ways. The limitations on the generalizability of focus group results have at least the advantage that convenience sampling can be employed. Indeed, convenience sampling is the most common method for selecting participants in focus groups. This type of sampling saves both time and money, but it does not eliminate the need to consider the characteristics of the group. The intent of virtually all focus groups is to draw some conclusions about a population of interest, so the group must consist of representative members of the larger population. If the research question is related to the responses of specific types of individuals (e.g., men, children, physicians), the composition of the group must reflect this type of individual. In addition, it may be desirable in some situations to have a group that is made up of a particular mix of people (e.g., older and younger individuals, men and women, users and nonusers of a particular product or service). Thus, convenience sampling does not free the researcher from matching the sample used in the focus group to the objectives of the research.

Further, as we saw in previous chapters, the composition of the group has important implications for the outcome of the discussion. Insofar as the researcher has a specific agenda and wishes the group to interact in particular ways, he or she will structure the membership of the group to maximize the probability of the desired outcome. This may mean ensuring a certain level of homogeneity/heterogeneity within the group or carrying out multiple groups that differ with respect to their composition.

Many types of focus groups require only very generally defined groups of individuals. For example, in many marketing research applications, the group may be defined simply in terms of the principal food shopper in a household or the user of a particular product. Government planners may define groups in terms of individuals who are likely to be affected by a new program or regulation. When such general definitions of the group are used, recruitment is relatively easy.

Many civic and religious organizations make their memberships available for focus group recruitment. Lists of individuals who have certain characteristics or who have engaged in certain types of activities also may be readily available. For example, many organizations maintain lists of their members, employees, or customers. Persons who have recently purchased homes or automobiles can be identified easily by examining court or tax records. When such lists are available, they save considerable time and expense because they reduce the number of contacts that must be made in order to identify individuals who are appropriate for the group. Marketing research companies and professional focus group facilities commonly maintain extensive databases from which they select focus group participants.

When preexisting lists are not available, the only alternative is to contact individuals by telephone, by mail, e-mail, or through intercepting them in public places. The same types of procedures used to identify and qualify participants that are employed in survey research are ordinarily used in such instances. For example, random-digit dialing procedures may be employed to identify representative households. Then a few brief screening questions can be used to determine whether individuals meet the requirements for participation in a particular focus group. Further information concerning the recruitment of representative samples can be found in Fowler (2002) in this series.

A particularly helpful reference for identifying focus group facilities and service providers, including organizations that can assist with recruiting, is the *Directory of Focus Group Companies and Services*. This directory provides information about companies and services around the world. It is also available online at www.greenbook.org/. A similar resource can be found at www.quirks .com/focus/search_focus_geo.asp.

Making Contact

The first step in recruiting a focus group is screening eligibility. The initial contact may occur by mail, e-mail, telephone, or in person. When the researcher's purpose requires that groups be composed in a particular way, a few qualifying questions may be used. These questions may include demographic characteristics, personality factors, or other variables related to the purpose of the research. When multiple groups need to be carried out, with different groups composed in different ways, this type of screening is necessary for matching individuals with specific groups.

After it has been determined that the individual contacted is appropriate for participation, the individual is usually given a general description of the nature of research, including the fact that the research will involve a group discussion. The general topic for research should be identified and the importance of the individual's participation and opinions should be emphasized. If an incentive is to be used, this should be indicated along with how and when it will be paid. If refreshments or a meal are to be served, this too should be noted.

Prospective participants should then be given the time and place of the group. Both the starting and ending times for the group should be indicated. It is a good idea to ask group members to arrive 15–30 minutes prior to the interview in order to account for traffic delays, weather conditions, and other assorted minor emergencies. One advantage of scheduling several focus groups on the same topic is that the participant can be offered several alternative times, dates, and often locations. Such alternatives increase the likelihood that an individual will be free to participate.

Once individuals have agreed to participate in a focus group, they should immediately receive either a written confirmation or a confirming telephone call. Written confirmations are preferable when time permits because they provide a means for delivering a map and directions to the site of the discussion. Written confirmations also carry a more formal tone and imply an obligation that serves to increase the commitment of the individual to participate.

Regardless of the type of confirmation used, participants should be contacted again by telephone 24 hours prior to the focus group. This reminds the participant of the earlier agreement and provides an opportunity to ensure that the participant has accurate directions.

Incentives

Focus groups are a time-consuming activity for participants. Taking 2 or more hours out of one's life to talk to a group of strangers is not the most appealing prospect, particularly if one has worked all day. There are a variety of incentives that may be used to encourage participation, and most focus group participants are provided monetary and other incentives (e.g., product samples or a chance to win a prize). In addition, for most people, the focus group itself is an incentive because it is generally an enjoyable experience. When recruiting participants, this aspect of participation should be emphasized. A stimulating discussion is not enough to induce most individuals to spend time in a focus group, however. Commercial research organizations pay focus group participants a range of incentives depending on the nature of the group sought and how difficult they are to recruit. Compensation can range from $50 to several hundred dollars for participation.

It is also a good idea to serve snacks or even a light meal if the group will be conducted near a mealtime. The presence of food tends to relax participants, and it encourages participation by eliminating concerns about meals. Food is not always appropriate and may be out of place in some international venues. Child care services also help ensure participation.

Other types of incentives that have been used include providing free products, transportation, and even overnight hotel accommodations. Incentives should be selected that have universal value to the participants. What may be valuable to one person may have little value to other. This is one reason money is most commonly employed.

Providing membership lists is a common fund-raising activity for many civic and religious organizations. Such organizations provide the researcher with a ready-made list of individuals who have agreed, at least in principle, to serve as research subjects. The disadvantage of using such groups, however, is that many of the individuals may be well known to one another or even close friends. Such individuals may form small cliques within the group and reinforce the opinions of one another. This may diminish the responsiveness of other group members or move the group toward a consensus opinion more quickly than might otherwise be the case. Friends are more likely to engage in side conversations that may disrupt the flow of discussion in the group or create resentment among others in the group. As we saw in Chapter 2, the dynamics of groups change radically depending on the level of acquaintanceship and the homogeneity of the participants. It is generally not desirable to have a few people who know one another well within a group of strangers. Further, a group composed of rather homogeneous friends is likely to produce less variance in opinion than a group of strangers, who might otherwise be equally homogeneous.

In addition, over time, such groups tend to become professional focus group participants. Such "professionals" are seldom representative of the larger population. For these reasons, it is a good idea to inquire how frequently the available individuals participate in focus group activities. Prospective participants can also be screened to ensure that they have not recently participated in other focus groups and are not acquainted with other participants.

Location

Chapter 2 noted that focus groups may take place in a wide variety of settings and reviewed many of the factors related to location that may influence the dynamics of a group's interaction and discussion. This review suggests that location is an important factor to consider when designing a group. Location will also influence the ease with which participants are recruited. In general, the closer the location to participants' homes or work, the more likely they are to participate. Travel time is generally more critical than distance in determining convenience, and when the location of the interview can take place between home and work, there is less a sense of traveling out of one's way.

Location also has psychological implications. Many prospective participants may be reluctant to travel to a location in a seedy part of town or to a deserted downtown location. Focus groups held in familiar, well-traveled areas are likely to be perceived as more attractive. This is one reason why shopping malls are a favored location by many researchers. Shopping malls are familiar, well-traveled, and attractive locations in which focus group participants feel comfortable. They also serve to set the tone of the focus group as an interesting experience and provide a set of cues for participants that suggest professionalism, comfort, and purpose.

How Many Participants?

Most focus groups are composed of 6 to 12 people. Fewer than 6 participants makes for a rather dull discussion, and more than 12 participants are difficult for the moderator to manage. The presence of more than a dozen participants also does not afford enough opportunity for all individuals to actively participate. It is generally a good idea to recruit more individuals than required, however. A good rule of thumb is to assume that at least 2 participants will not show up for the interview. This number may vary somewhat depending on the nature of the participants and the type of recruitment used. For example, participants who have significant demands on their time, like senior executives and physicians, are often required to make last-minute schedule changes that may result in their missing a focus group meeting. Individuals who must travel a long distance through heavy traffic may be delayed, even if they had planned to attend the session. On the other hand, participants who are recruited through a local civic organization for a group that will be conducted in a location a few blocks from their homes are much more likely to attend the group.

It is generally better to overrecruit slightly than to cancel a group because too few individuals are present. If by some chance all participants who were recruited do happen to show up, it is relatively easy to ask one or two persons to leave. Most often the best way to do this is to ask the last persons to arrive to leave. The incentive should always be provided, even when the participant is asked to leave.

The question of how many is related to the number of focus groups as well as the number of persons in each group. There are no general rules concerning the optimal number of groups. When the research is very complex or when numerous different types of individuals are of interest, more focus groups will be required. When the population of interest is relatively homogeneous and the research question is relatively simple, a single group or two may be sufficient. Exceptions do occur, however. In 2000, *Newsweek* magazine reported Airbus's fielding of over 120 focus groups to help design their new A3XX jumbo jet (A. Bryant & Emerson, 2000). Most focus group applications involve more than one group, but seldom more than three or four groups. The question of the number of groups to use is ultimately one that must be determined based on the objectives of the research. It is also a question that must be informed by the factors reviewed in Chapter 3 because the dynamics of individual groups may well be related to the purpose of the research.

Recruiting Hard to Reach Individuals

There are occasions when a particular research question requires that focus group discussions be carried out with individuals who are difficult to reach.

Such individuals include physicians, senior business executives, government officials, and an array of other specialists or just very busy people. Recruiting such individuals for participation in focus groups is not impossible, but it may require heroic efforts. In many cases, it may also be found that individual interviews are easier and less costly to schedule. Nevertheless, focus groups have been and can be carried out with such people.

One way to reach individuals who are otherwise difficult to recruit is to go to places where they tend to congregate. Trade shows, professional conventions and conferences, and business meetings are often good places to recruit and carry out focus groups. Groups may be recruited prior to the event or on site. Generally, such groups will feature a cocktail party or other event for the participants. Some organizations have gone so far as to sponsor their own conferences, often in attractive locations, just to obtain access to such individuals.

Incentives are generally not required to obtain participation in such settings. Focus groups with business executives are often easier to schedule in airports than other places. Airports are places where some people spend a significant amount of time simply waiting and where an interview or focus group may provide a way to fill some time.

Physicians may often be recruited more readily if the location of the interview is a hospital at which they practice. In some cases, it may be necessary to compensate them at their hourly rate in order to obtain access.

One particularly creative telecommunications company decided that it needed to talk with the chief executive officers of major corporations. Such individuals tend to be extremely busy and are virtually impossible to find in the same place. The telecommunications firm made an offer too good to resist. It chartered a cruise ship and invited the CEOs and their spouses for a 3-day weekend cruise, all expenses paid. The firm succeeded in drawing over 200 CEOs to the cruise. Although the cruise cost several hundred thousand dollars, it was well worth the cost to have a captive research pool for 3 days.

In recent years, working mothers with young children have increasingly become a difficult group to interview. Providing babysitting services is almost a requirement for obtaining their participation. Holding the focus group in a shopping mall location and extending the babysitting service for an hour or so before or after the focus group provides an additional incentive for participation.

The key to recruiting any group is an understanding of where and how potential group members spend their time, what barriers may exist that make participation difficult, and what incentives are valued by the group. This understanding provides a basis for developing a recruitment plan that includes a location that optimizes participation and the identification of ways to eliminate barriers and provide incentives for participation in a focus group.

It is important to remember that the greatest obstacle to carrying out a focus group is the need to bring 8 to 12 people together at the same place and time. Time is a finite resource in modern society: The time budget of the average individual may be more constrained than the financial budget. Asking individuals to spend 90 minutes to 2 hours in a focus group discussion—plus time traveling to and from the group—is asking for a significant sacrifice on the part of the individual. Rearranging their calendars, forgoing dinner, finding babysitters, or traveling to unfamiliar locations is simply too great a sacrifice for many potential focus group members. In fact, growing "time poverty" raises some concerns about the lifestyle representativeness of individuals who do show up for focus groups.

The researcher should be sensitive to and appreciative of the sacrifice participants make. A $50 incentive is not very much for a 3-hour detour on the way home from work, particularly if a babysitter for the children costs $10 an hour. Researcher arrogance may be the single most important factor in the failure of a focus group. Participants are doing the researcher—and his or her sponsors—a favor, regardless of the compensation and other incentives provided. Recognition of this fact—and an appreciation of the participants' potential sacrifices—is a good beginning for scheduling a focus group.

DEVELOPING THE INTERVIEW GUIDE

The interview guide sets the agenda for a focus group discussion. It should grow directly from the research questions that were the impetus for the research. Like the selection and recruitment of participants, the construction of the interview guide should not proceed until the research agenda and all of the questions related to it have been clearly articulated and agreed on by all parties with an interest in the research.

The development of the interview guide is not typically the sole responsibility of the focus group moderator. Indeed, the moderator may not even be selected until the research agenda has been established and a preliminary interview guide has been drafted. The interview guide should be developed in collaboration with all parties interested in the research at hand. These include policy and decision makers who may use the information, as well as the researchers charged with implementing the research. At some point, the moderator should be brought into the design process as well to ensure that he or she is comfortable with the instrument and understands the intent of the questions.

When designing an interview guide, it is important to remember that its purpose is to provide direction for the group discussion. It is critical to recognize that a focus group interview discussion guide is not a verbal version of a survey questionnaire. Survey questionnaires provide a great deal more structure than should a focus group interview guide because they serve different purposes. In addition, survey questionnaires often provide both questions and potential responses from which the research participant selects an answer. Interview guides provide far less structure in the questions themselves and do not suggest potential responses.

Formulating Questions

Along with the composition of the group, a key element in the design of a successful focus group is the formulation of questions. Questions serve as the agenda for the group discussion, and a good question will elicit substantial interaction among group members. There is a rich literature on how to develop good questions. Perhaps the best book ever written on the topic of question development is *The Art of Asking Questions* (Payne, 1951). Other useful sources include Sudman and Bradburn (1982), Schaeffer and Presser (2003), and the several practical guides to focus group research referenced elsewhere in this book.

When developing the interview guide, there are two general principles that should be observed. The first suggests that questions be ordered from the more general to the more specific. This means that questions of the most general and unstructured nature should be placed early, and more specific questions, which may suggest specific responses to the more general questions, should be placed near the end of the guide. Second, questions should be ordered by the relative importance to the research agenda. Thus, the questions of greatest importance should be placed early, near the top of the guide, whereas those of lesser significance should be placed near the end.

These two principles may appear to conflict, and they often do, but it is frequently possible to establish an agenda that starts with general questions about one particular topic, moves to specific questions about this topic, and then moves back to another general question. Obviously, this approach does not work well when the topics for discussion are very closely related and when the answers to specific questions regarding one topic may influence the response to the more general questions to be raised later.

Ultimately the researcher will need to exercise judgment in making trade-offs between the general-to-specific rule and the most-to-least-important rule. In some cases, when there are many questions of high importance, the only solution may be the use of a number of different focus groups, each with its own interview guide. Further, it is important to recognize that groups often take on a life of their own, and the agenda is dictated by the natural flow of discussion. Thus, the interview guide is just that—a *guide*—that the moderator and group should be allowed to modify if it proves desirable. This might occur when two groups are scheduled and a line of questioning doesn't "work" for one group, which leads to its rephrasing or the elimination of these questions for the second group.

Another factor that must be considered in the design of the interview guide is the amount of effort required to discuss a particular topic. It is virtually impossible to extend any group beyond 2 hours without exhausting everyone, but some topics create cognitive fatigue more quickly than others. Very technical topics or topics that are emotionally charged will exhaust participants more quickly, and the interview guide should reflect this fact. When the topic is likely to require considerable energy and effort on the part of the participants, the interview guide should be shorter and involve fewer questions.

How Many Questions?

It is often difficult to judge the number of topics and questions that can be covered in a designated amount of time. Different groups will spend radically different amounts of time on the same topics, and what may evolve as a long and intense discussion in one group may be met with disinterest by another group. Chapter 2 reviewed some of the factors that might influence the amount of time required to deal with particular topics by groups of varying composition. A very homogeneous group may be able to move through many questions quickly, whereas a group composed of very heterogeneous individuals on a number of dimensions may labor over even a small number of questions. An experienced moderator can often provide some guidance with respect to the amount of material that can be covered on a particular topic. Generally, the more complex a topic, the more emotionally involving the topic, or the greater the heterogeneity of views on the topic within the group, the fewer the topics and specific questions that can be covered.

In practice, most interview guides consist of fewer than a dozen questions, although the moderator is frequently given considerable latitude to probe responses and add new questions as the actual interview progresses. A focus group interview is a dynamic and idiosyncratic exercise, so such flexibility in pursuing new questions is critical to the success of the interview. It may be helpful during the design of the interview guide to try to anticipate the many directions in which a discussion will go. This is often not practical, however, because one reason for carrying out a focus group is the lack of information regarding the topic for discussion.

One option available to the researcher who carries out several focus groups is the *rolling interview guide*. As suggested earlier, an interview guide is developed for the first group. Then, based on the outcome of the first group discussion, the guide is revised for use in the second group. Information obtained in the second group may then be used for yet another revision of the interview, and the whole process repeated. This process may continue until a guide is developed with which the researcher is comfortable or until interviews with all groups have been completed. One significant disadvantage associated with this approach, however, is that it makes comparison across groups even more difficult. With the use of rolling interview guides, no group is asked to respond to exactly the same set of questions. Despite this disadvantage, a rolling interview guide may be the only alternative available and frequently makes the best use of multiple focus groups because it allows information to unfold over time as more is discovered about a topic.

How Much Structure?

It was noted earlier that questions in the interview guide should not be survey-like and structured to provide potential responses for the discussants; yet even when such highly structured questions are avoided, there remains considerable choice regarding the amount of structure to use when designing questions. Although it is impossible to completely eliminate structure in questions, it is possible and often desirable to design relatively unstructured questions. Such relatively open questions allow respondents to refer to virtually any aspect of the general stimulus identified in the question. The degree of response freedom is high. For example, a relatively unstructured question might take one of the following forms:

How do you feel about XYZ?

What thoughts went through your head while you watched the program?

What did you think about when you first saw XYZ?

Note that these questions do not draw attention to any specific aspect or dimension of the stimulus object referred to in the question. Respondents can select any aspect or dimension, and, indeed, what they select may have important implications. More specifically, those issues that respondents raise first are likely to be those that are most memorable, important, or salient to them. Exceptions to this general rule are topics that are threatening or of a very sensitive or potentially embarrassing nature.

Structure may be introduced into a question by providing information about those dimensions or aspects of the stimulus object on which the respondent should focus. Thus, a question may ask respondents about a particular dimension of the stimulus object in the question:

Do you think a value-added tax will help the very rich or the very poor?

How do you feel about the safety of X automobile?

When do you use your widget?

Alternatively, the question may draw attention to a particular stimulus object:

How did you feel about the woman in the perfume ad?

Did you find the spokesperson believable?

What did you learn from the advertisement that you didn't know before?

Generally, the less structured types of questions will precede those with more structure, because those with more structure tend to be more directive and establish a direction for response. Although more structured questions do not suggest a specific answer, they do tend to move the discussion in a particular direction and narrow its scope.

Although it may appear that less structure is better in focus group interviews, this is not always the case. Some people need help in articulating a response. Providing a key word or cue may help the respondent formulate an answer. In other cases, those aspects of the stimulus object that are most salient and easily remembered for respondents may not be aspects of primary interest to the researcher. This often occurs in communication research when the researcher may be interested in the full array of beliefs and feelings communicated, but the respondent is able to recall only the most salient aspects of the communication. More specific cues—aspects of the communication—may be required to elicit less salient or memorable portions of the communication. On the other hand, it is important that the interviewer not lead the respondent, in the sense of providing an answer.

Rephrasing a question can be helpful, but suggesting what the respondent should say is not appropriate. A skillful moderator is often able to handle this problem by having other group members interpret or rephrase the question. This is not always a viable solution, however, because another group member may simply be suggesting an answer. Even so, this is more desirable because the other group members are less aware than the moderator of the research agenda.

A critical issue in determining the amount of structure is the preservation of the emic mode of data collection referred to in Chapter 3. Focus groups are designed to determine how respondents structure the world, not how participants respond to the researcher's view of how the world or a particular phenomenon is structured.

More structured questions may be useful when respondents are uncertain or embarrassed about a particular response. Even when an aspect of the stimulus object or response to the object is very salient, it may not be offered as part of a response to a relatively unstructured question for fear of being wrong or embarrassed. Such situations benefit from skillful moderator probing. Also, providing additional structure may serve to bring out such responses by suggesting an interest in the topic and by communicating that such responses are acceptable.

Because the objective of a focus group is to stimulate discussion, questions that call for a direct, one- or two-word response should be avoided. Questions that can be answered simply "yes" or "no" provide little information and stifle discussion. Although closed-ended questions of the agree-disagree variety—or questions that suggest specific sets of responses—may be particularly appropriate in survey research, they are of little use in focus group research. Questions that include words like *how, why, under what conditions,* and similar probes suggest to respondents that the researcher is interested in complexity and wants to facilitate discussion. On the other hand, an occasional group "vote" can elevate the group energy and provide a basis for continued elaborated discussion.

The form and characteristics of the questions are not the only determinant of the amount of structure in a focus group discussion. The style and personality of the moderator, as well as the composition of the group itself, also influences the amount of structure and its desirability. Thus, we will return to the issue of structure in Chapters 5 and 6 when we examine the influence of the moderator and the ways in which focus groups may be conducted.

Wording of Questions

Respondents can give meaningful responses only to questions they understand. This means that questions should be phrased simply in language that respondents understand. Long, complex, multipart questions are not only difficult to understand but also difficult to respond to and irritating to the group.

The way in which questions are worded may also place respondents in an embarrassing or defensive situation. This should be avoided, and in most circumstances, questions can be phrased to avoid threatening or embarrassing the respondent. For example, "Why don't you take your child in for a regular checkup with a doctor?" is a potentially embarrassing question. The same question might be asked as follows: "What prevents you from taking your child to the doctor as often as you would like?" It may even be possible for the moderator to have other group members raise these questions or play off of the responses of the group in such a way as to place the question within the natural flow of the discussion. This often reduces the anxiety or embarrassment of a respondent, and a skillful moderator will know when to use this technique to broach a topic rather than ask a question directly. In these situations, indirect projective techniques often prove useful in eliciting data about sensitive topics. A little forethought and sensitivity go a long way toward the prevention of embarrassing and threatening questions and may make the difference between a lively, talkative group and one that is sullen and uncomfortably quiet.

Pretesting

There is no substitute for trying out an interview guide prior to its use. No matter how experienced the researcher and moderator and how thorough and conscientious the designers, it is impossible to predict in advance the way respondents will interpret and respond to questions. Professional researchers are not typical individuals, and no matter how skilled, their articulation of questions is not usually representative of the research population. This means that at least some degree of pretesting is appropriate. Such pretesting may take a variety of forms ranging from a small mock focus group to simply trying out the questions on a few individuals. At minimum, those persons involved in the pretest should not have been involved in the design of the interview guide and should not be aware of the purpose of the research. When practical, it is highly desirable to carry out the pretesting with respondents who are representative of those who will participate in the actual focus groups.

Pretesting of the interview guide provides an opportunity to determine whether wording of questions is appropriate, to determine whether questions elicit discussion, and to identify questions that are not easily understood. It should be noted, however, that the interview guide is only one part of the research instrument; the group itself and the moderator are also parts of the research instrument. This means it is impossible to fully pretest the total research instrument outside a group setting.

ISSUES AND TRENDS FOR THE FUTURE

Decisions about the number of focus group participants and the number and type of questions to be addressed in the group are separate considerations, yet they inevitably interact and exert strong influences about the quality and effectiveness of the group discussion. In the marketing research field where as much as a billion dollars are spent annually on focus groups, three trends related to these issues have had the effect of encouraging focus groups that are very different from their theoretical origins and design. First, the time poverty of both managers and participants has resulted in a slow creep toward shorter, down-to-business *focus groups* that wrap things up quickly. This is not necessarily harmful by itself, but it has occurred at the same time that managers have significantly increased the workload of a typical focus group. Naomi

Henderson (2004) estimates that compared with a few decades ago, moderators today commonly have to cover twice as many questions in the same amount of time. This has had a chilling effect on the overall quality of focus groups. Moderators who have to wade through 35–40 questions in 75 minutes are likely to feel (and look) rushed and are highly unlikely to probe participants' responses. The group members quickly pick up the idea that it's best to provide relatively terse reactions and help move things forward. Focus groups that materialize this way are actually closer to within-group surveys than focused group depth interviews. Rook (2003) provides a framework for better understanding *in advance* the tradeoffs involved in selecting the number of questions, participants, and allocated time.

Finally, focus group discussion guides tend to rely largely on direct questions about consumers' purchase behavior, motivations, and perceptions. These are important issues, but in many situations, consumers are unlikely to be able or willing to provide the desired information. Many questions are sensitive, potentially embarrassing, or affected by social desirability influences, so focus group respondents may resist answering or distort their responses. Also, as Gerald Zaltman (2003) demonstrates in his book, *How Customers Think,* individuals may simply be unable verbally to express deep-seated feelings and nonverbal images. In recent years, a spike in uses of projective research methods (in both group and individual interviews) owes much to their distinctive strengths in eliciting *indirectly* data about such topics.

CONCLUSION

The selection and recruitment of participants for a focus group is a critical part of the design process. The fact that focus groups are not designed to produce projectable statistical results does not mean that care should be abandoned when recruiting respondents. As in all research, respondents should be selected from an identified population of relevance to the research question. Likewise, the interview guide should be designed with care and with a clear understanding of the research problem.

Focus groups are not random discussions among a group of individuals who are brought together haphazardly. Rather, they are group discussions among carefully selected individuals guided by a skilled moderator who follows a well-constructed but loose and flexible interview guide. Ultimately, the composition of the group, the structure of the interview guide, and the location of the interview must flow from a well-defined research objective. Like all other research, focus group research begins with and should be guided by a well-articulated purpose.

REVIEW QUESTIONS

1. Why is the establishment of the research agenda, or research question, the first step necessary in both recruiting focus group participants and designing an interview guide?

2. Why is convenience sampling the most common type of sampling employed in selecting respondents for a focus group? What are the relative advantages and disadvantages of this approach to recruiting participants?

3. Why must attention be paid to the composition of focus groups? What factors should be considered when determining the composition of a particular group?

4. What steps may a researcher take to ensure the participation of potential group members?

5. What types of individuals are difficult to recruit for participation in focus groups? Why? For each group identified, list some ways to increase the probability of their participation.

6. What is the purpose of a focus group interview guide? How does such a guide differ from a survey questionnaire? What are the reasons for this difference?

7. What are the two principal rules governing the design of an interview guide? How does one resolve conflicts between these two principles?

8. What is a "rolling" interview guide? Why is it used? What are its advantages and disadvantages?

9. What is a relatively structured question? How should structure be introduced into a focus group question? Why is the use of structure necessary?

10. What factors should be considered when selecting the wording of questions used in the focus group interview guide? Why are these factors important?

11. Why is pretesting a necessary step in developing an interview guide? How would a researcher pretest an interview guide?

Exercise: Select a topic. Develop a description of the type of individuals you would include in a focus group discussion of this topic. Indicate how you would recruit such individuals. Develop an interview guide for a discussion of this topic.

5

The Focus Group Moderator

Throughout the first four chapters of the book, we have suggested that an effective moderator is one of the keys to the collection of rich and valid insights from focus groups. In this chapter, we examine the role of the moderator and consider issues related to his or her selection and training. In so doing, we draw on the substantial literature on interviewer effects and interviewing (cf. Fowler & Mangione, 1989). It is clear that what distinguishes the most effective focus group moderators from the others is a function of both individual and situational factors. These include personal characteristics (e.g., age, sex, personality); educational background and training; amount of experience as a moderator; and situational characteristics such as the sensitivity of the topic, the scope and depth of coverage required, the conduciveness of the physical setting, and time constraints. Mastering the technique of moderating a focus group is an art requiring a moderator to wear many hats and assume different roles during the course of even a single focus group. He or she has the unenviable task of balancing the requirements of sensitivity and empathy, on one hand, and objectivity and detachment on the other.

An important first question is whether a moderator should be selected on the basis of specific requirements related to the purpose of the group, the group's composition, and the location of the group or whether there exists an ideal general-purpose moderator who can handle most if not all focus group interviews. To answer this question, we need to examine what it takes to be a good moderator or facilitator and then see if these requirements or standards are representative of an individual or require an interaction of specific characteristics of the moderator with characteristics of the group. For example, Karger (1987) suggests the following:

> The best facilitator has unobtrusive chameleon-like qualities; gently draws consumers into the process; deftly encourages them to interact with one another for optimum synergy; lets the intercourse flow naturally with a minimum of intervention; listens openly and deeply; uses silence well; plays back consumer statements in a distilling way which brings out more refined thoughts or explanations; and remains completely non-authoritarian and non-judgmental.
>
> Yet the facilitator will subtly guide the proceeding when necessary and intervene to cope with various kinds of troublesome participants who may impair the productive group process. (p. 54)

D. N. Scott (1987) emphasizes that the choice of the moderator is critical and points out the following:

> Moderators have the difficult task of dealing with dynamics that constantly evolve during a focus group discussion. They must know how to handle the "rational man" syndrome, in which respondents give the "right" or "socially acceptable" answer.
>
> A good moderator must handle the problem by constantly checking behavior against attitudes, challenging and drawing out respondents with opposite views and looking for the emotional component of the responses. (p. 35)

Given these extensive expectations of moderators, let us now review some of the theoretical bases for the art of moderating. Insights on effective moderating can be drawn from three major research streams: interviewing techniques and tactics, leadership studies, and group dynamics. This knowledge together with an adequate understanding of the research problem can help improve the effectiveness of moderating in four ways: selection of the moderator, preparation of the moderator, the process of moderating, and analysis of focus group data (including evaluating the unintended consequences of moderator behavior).

This chapter focuses primarily on the application of interviewing principles and knowledge of leadership styles to moderator selection and preparation. The dynamics of moderating a focus group and the role of the moderator in the analysis of focus group data are discussed in greater detail in Chapter 6. We begin with a brief review of leadership styles and interviewing strategies and discuss their implications for different styles of moderating. This is followed by a discussion of the issues related to moderator training, preparation, and selection.

LEADERSHIP AND GROUP DYNAMICS

The focus group moderator is placed by default in the role of nominal leader of the group. Exactly what this role entails will vary from group to group, however. There are many interpretations of leadership. It has often been associated with motivation, exercise of social influence (power), giving direction, and providing a good example for others in the group. Pennington (2002) observes that it is important to distinguish between leader and leadership: "Leadership may be regarded as social influence; however, leaders occupy powerful positions in a group" (p. 125). Two classic definitions serve to illustrate the process nature of leadership:

Leadership is the process of influencing group activities toward goal setting and goal achievement. (Stogdill, 1950, p. 3)

Leadership is interpersonal influence, exercised in situation and directed, through the communication process, toward the attainment of a specified goal or goals. (Tannenbaum, Weschler, & Massarik, 1961, p. 24)

There is some communality among the numerous definitions of leadership: It involves people, influence, and goals. Certainly by these criteria, the focus group moderator is a leader. Carter (1954) in his classic study of leaders identified three broad clusters of traits related to leadership:

Group goal facilitation, which includes those abilities that are necessary to help the group attain its goal (e.g., insight, intelligence, knowing how to get things done)

Group sociability, which includes those factors that are necessary to keep the group functioning smoothly (e.g., sociability, cooperativeness, popularity)

Individual prominence, which includes factors related to the person's desire for group recognition (e.g., initiative, self-confidence, persistence) (pp. 477–484)

As pointed out in Chapter 2, the emergence of leadership is influenced by individual characteristics, such as personality and intelligence, and interpersonal processes, such as group cohesiveness, compatibility, and the homogeneity/ heterogeneity of the group. Furthermore, situational variables such as spatial position and location in the communication network can affect the probability of a person becoming a leader. For example, a person occupying a spatial position providing the maximum eye contact has a greater probability of emerging as a leader. Also, central positions in communication networks enhance leadership selection and emergence. Thus, the focus group moderator is not only the nominal leader of the group but is generally seated in a central position within the group, which tends to reinforce the leadership role. These factors alone, however, do not make the moderator a leader. Personal traits and behavior must reinforce the initial role designation or the moderator will lose his or her leadership position to others in the group.

The traditional approach to studying leadership, called the trait approach, has been based on the assumption that leaders possess certain traits or characteristics that distinguish them from nonleaders. Thus, one might expect focus group moderators to possess such traits. Stogdill (1948, 1974) reviewed almost 300 trait studies conducted between 1904 and 1970 and concluded that personal characteristics do contribute to successful leadership and that certain situational factors may determine which traits are important for leadership

TABLE 5.1
Traits and Skills Associated With Successful Leaders

Traits	Skills
Adaptable to situations	Clever (intelligent)
Alert to social environment	Conceptually skilled
Ambitious and achievement oriented	Creative
Assertive	Diplomatic and tactful
Cooperative	Fluent in speaking
Decisive	Knowledgeable about group task
Dependable	Organized (administrative ability)
Dominant (desire to influence others)	Persuasive
Energetic (high activity level)	Socially skilled
Persistent	Self-confident
Tolerant of stress	
Willing to assume responsibility	

SOURCE: From Yuki, G., *Leadership in Organizations, 2/e,* © 1981, p. 176. Reprinted by permission of Prentice Hall, Inc., Englewood Cliffs, NJ.

emergence and effectiveness. The traits and skills found to be associated with successful leadership, according to Stogdill's review, are summarized in Table 5.1, as compiled in Yukl (1981). Because the traits associated with successful leadership appear to be contingent on the situation, researchers have also looked at the effectiveness of different styles of leadership under various conditions (cf. Chemers, 2003; Fiedler, 1967; Forsyth, 2006; House & Mitchell, 1974; Peters, Hartke, & Pohlmann, 1985).

Because the focus group interview is a well-defined but temporally limited situation that is quite different from other natural social situations in which leadership may be important, the research on factors influencing leadership in specific types of situations is particularly relevant to the identification of successful focus group moderators. Especially relevant to this contingency notion of leadership is path-goal theory.

According to the path-goal theory of leadership (House & Baetz, 1979; House & Mitchell, 1974), a leader can increase motivation of his subordinates by clarifying the paths to rewards and/or by increasing rewards. There are different ways to go about doing this. Four kinds of leadership behaviors or styles have been identified that vary according to two situational factors: group member characteristics and work environment characteristics. Group members may differ according to their motivation, abilities, self-confidence, and willingness to work together. The situation itself can be either structured or unstructured. Accordingly, one of the following styles would be more appropriate (Pennington, 2002, p. 145):

Supportive leadership. Show concern for the well being and personal needs of subordinates, be friendly and approachable, be considerate, create a friendly climate, and treat group members as equals.

Directive leadership. Tell subordinates what they are expected to do, give guidance and direction, provide standards and schedules, set performance targets, and ask group members to follow rules and regulations.

Participative leadership. Consult with group members about activities, schedules, and targets; ask for opinions and suggestions; allow for participation in decision making; and take group members' views into account.

Achievement-oriented leadership. Set challenging goals, seek improvement in performance, emphasize excellence in performance, and show expectation and confidence that group members have the ability to attain high standards.

The primary responsibility and challenge for a leader is, therefore, to analyze the requirements of the task and characteristics of the group and adopt the appropriate leadership style that would be most effective for accomplishing the task. Moderators of focus groups are no different from other types of leaders in this respect. In fact, their leadership task can be viewed as more challenging. They are dealing with strangers most of the time, and they have little power (in the traditional sense) to influence participants. Although a work manager can always appeal to the reward structure to encourage productivity, moderators of focus groups have to use persuasion and tact to encourage group participation and maintain interest in the topic. Thus, the leadership style most appropriate for a successful focus group moderator is likely to be of the supportive nature, though certain groups may require other types of styles. It is not clear that individuals move easily from one leadership style to another, so there may be occasions when a moderator will need to be matched with a given group based on his or her leadership style.

INTERVIEWING STYLES AND TACTICS

A substantial amount of literature on interviewing principles and practices, communication styles, and questioning strategies can be found in fields such as counseling and psychotherapy, personnel management, communication, and marketing research. Stewart and Cash (2002), for example, identify and discuss at least five major types of interviewing: informational, persuasive, employment, appraisal, and counseling. Each is similar in terms of the need to follow certain communication principles and strategies but differs in terms of the basic objective and use of the interview data.

Focus groups, as discussed in Chapters 1 and 3, have different uses, and as such, the interviewing style, the type of questions, and the amount of interaction desired among participants will vary according to the purpose. Further, as noted in Chapter 2, the composition of a group may necessitate a particular style of interviewing, and most certainly, the purpose of a group will determine the style of interviewing required. For example, a less structured and freewheeling approach to focus groups would be desirable if the purpose is to generate new ideas or encourage creativity. On the other hand, a more structured approach with occasional in-depth probing may be required when the objective of the interview is to generate research hypotheses or to diagnose potential problems with a new program, product, or service, particularly when the topic is sensitive or potentially embarrassing. We return to the issue of structure in Chapter 6.

Questions play an important role, not only in getting at answers to the research problem but also in setting the tone or climate for interaction. As we noted in earlier chapters, the opening questions in a group interview can put participants either at ease or on the defensive. Stewart and Cash (2002) and Churchill and Iacobucci (2004) provide a detailed discussion of different types of questions and their uses. Basically, questions fall into one of two categories: open or closed. *Open-ended questions* tend to be broader in nature and allow the respondent a great deal of freedom to provide the amount of information he or she wants to give. Thus, the following are all examples of open-ended questions:

What do you think are the biggest problems with the local public transportation system?

What steps might be taken to improve the quality of your local schools?

What factors are important in your decision to buy a particular make and model of a car?

Closed-ended questions are more restrictive and tend to limit the answer options available to the respondent. Closed-ended questions either explicitly or implicitly provide answers from which respondents choose. For example, *explicit closed-ended questions* take the following form:

Do you agree or disagree that there is too much violence on television?

Is the amount of your copayment important or unimportant in your selection of a health care provider?

On a scale of 1 to 10, where 1 is poor and 10 is excellent, how would you rate the performance of your bank?

Implicit closed-ended questions do not suggest specific answers but carry a strong implication of limited choices from which respondents will choose. Implicit closed-ended questions include questions like these:

For whom do you plan to vote in the presidential election in November?

How many children do you have who are living at home?

Both open-ended and closed-ended questions may be appropriate in a focus group interview, but closed-ended questions in focus groups are more often used as the basis for polarizing opinion for further discussion than for closing discussion of the topic. Thus, a moderator might ask for a specific opinion regarding a topic as a means for demonstrating that the group does not agree. This initial polarization of the group can be used to create interest and provide a foundation for a more in-depth discussion of the reasons for the disagreement.

There is a trade-off in terms of the amount and reliability of the information generated through the use of open-ended versus closed-ended questions. The amount of data obtained tends to increase with the openness of the questions. However, the reliability of the data and the possibility of replication decrease as the questions become more open-ended. This may not be a serious concern for much focus group research, however. In survey research, where reliability and replicability are critical, there is a greater need to increase structure in the questions and constrain the variety of responses. In focus group interviews, the usefulness of information is more frequently gauged by the ability to draw valid conclusions about the topic under discussion than by the ability to replicate findings across many focus groups, however. Thus, less structure may be most appropriate for many applications.

We can also classify questions as primary and secondary. *Primary questions* are designed to help introduce topics in an interview or new areas within a topic and tend to be open-ended. *Secondary questions* can be either open-ended or closed-ended and are designed to follow up primary questions or probe in greater detail answers given to primary questions. Both types of questions play an important role in the focus group interview. Generally, focus group discussions start with primary questions and move to secondary questions.

Another important distinction is between directed (loaded) and neutral questions. In comparison with neutral questions, *directed questions* tend to pressure or force respondents to answer in a directed manner or choose one answer over another. According to Stewart and Cash (2002), the direction provided by the interviewer or moderator may be "intentional or unintentional, implicit or explicit, verbal or nonverbal" (p. 87). Directed or leading questions can be distinguished from neutral questions by evaluating the context and manner in which they are asked. Leading questions may be valuable when the intent is to probe into sensitive topics—such as alcohol abuse—when respondents tend to adopt a neutral stance in replying to questions or when there is a need to push respondents beyond simple or surface responses. Although such questions are sometimes necessary, too frequent use tends to place respondents in a reactive mode in which they simply respond to the interviewer's questions rather than generate their own freewheeling ideas in response to one another. This, in turn, tends to shift the research perspective from a more emic view to one that is largely etic.

As we noted in earlier chapters, the structure of questions is in large measure dictated by whether the emic or etic perspective is adopted. Focus groups generally utilize the emic perspective, which often sacrifices reliability and statistical projectability for a more dependable understanding of the idiographic processes that give rise to respondents' opinions and feelings. The contingencies and qualifications of opinions and attitudes that often accompany discussions in focus groups are often lost in surveys that require simple agree/disagree responses. On the other hand, the nuances of such qualifications make it difficult to draw firm conclusions about attitudes. There are, then, inevitable trade-offs in selecting one style of interviewing or mode of questioning over another. Ultimately, the style selected must match the purpose of the research.

Another aspect of interviewing style is the sequence in which questions are asked. Although it is most common to begin questioning with a more general question and move to more specific questions, this is not always the most appropriate approach. The interviewer or moderator may pursue any of several potential sequences of questions (cf. Stewart & Cash, 2002). Certain sequencing strategies may be more appropriate than others, and the choice of a sequence may vary with the topic and availability of time. Furthermore, there may be a need to adopt more than one sequencing strategy for different subtopics within a single interview or for different types of groups based on the anticipated or revealed dynamics of the groups.

The *funnel* approach to questioning, as the name implies, begins with broad questions followed by gradually more narrow questions. It is generally most appropriate for topics that are considered fairly sensitive and when the interviewees are quite knowledgeable but need more time and freedom to express themselves in the beginning of the interview before they can be effectively probed. In the *inverted funnel* sequence, closed questions are followed by increasingly more open-ended questions. The objective is to gradually motivate respondents to talk more freely about the subject. Opening questions are designed to assist the interviewee by either aiding recall or making it easier for him or her to answer.

The *quantamensional design* approach (Gallup, 1947) was developed to determine the intensity of respondents' opinions and attitudes. It involves a five-step approach, with questions designed to measure the following:

1. The degree of awareness
2. Uninfluenced attitudes
3. Specific attitudes
4. Reasons for these attitudes
5. Intensity of these attitudes

For example, in the context of an interview on disposal of hazardous chemical waste, the questions might be as follows:

1. What do you know about current methods of disposing hazardous chemical waste?
2. What, if any, are the factors that contribute to the growing stockpile of hazardous chemical waste?
3. Do you approve or disapprove of these methods of disposing hazardous chemical wastes?
4. Why do you feel that way?
5. How strongly do you feel about this—strongly, very strongly, something that you would not change your mind on?

Like the funnel and inverted funnel approach, this sequence of questions allows for a great deal of probing. This approach tends to move from a very general discussion of what the respondents know about a topic to their general opinions and feelings about a topic to respondents' attitudes and feelings about specific dimensions of the topic.

In contrast, the *tunnel* sequence is designed to get at interviewees' attitudes or opinions in a manner that will facilitate quantifying the data. It involves asking a series of similar questions in which respondents have to rate people, objects, or places. Little probing is possible under the tunnel approach because probing may influence subsequent ratings. This latter type of approach has more in common with traditional survey interviewing strategies than traditional approaches to focus group interviewing. Nevertheless, such interview strategies may be appropriate in certain situations.

The behavior of the moderator within the group communication network can strongly influence the effectiveness of different interviewing styles. When the objective of the focus group is to encourage ideas, a one-on-one interaction would tend to stifle creativity. The more productive approach would be to get all participants to feed off each other with the moderator's role being "relegated" to that of being one of the discussants, with occasional clarifying or directional questions. On the other hand, the moderator may need to take a more directive approach when the research agenda includes many very specific questions.

The positioning of moderator within the group also affects the kind of leadership influence that can be exerted on group participants. When greater direction or focus is desired, being central in the communication network would be more likely to facilitate the exercise of moderator influence than would being on the periphery of the network.

In short, leadership style and interviewing strategies go hand in hand to produce effective moderating. The appropriate leadership style often dictates the effectiveness of interviewing strategies. Different topics require different styles of moderating. Therefore, it is important to ensure that moderating style and ability are compatible with the demands (scope and depth requirements) of the research topic.

MODERATOR SELECTION

A useful starting point for selecting a moderator is to examine his or her personal characteristics (e.g., age, sex, personality), educational background and training, and amount of moderating experience. Generally, certain types of educational backgrounds—marketing, psychology, or other social sciences, or training in psychotherapy—are useful preparation for a moderator. These requirements are not necessary or even sufficient qualifications for effective moderating, however. Individuals with similar training and background often vary in moderating styles, which are largely shaped by personality factors. Langer (1978) noted that "moderating is essentially a creative art which must be practiced by those with a certain 'flair.' These talents relate not just to years of training but to something deeper" (p. 10). She highlights nine characteristics of good qualitative researchers, which are a function of both personality and training. These are summarized in Table 5.2. Collectively, these personal qualities suggest that many individuals would *not* make good moderators, and they also explain why so many moderators are women (Ivy & Backlund, 1994; Stewart & Cash, 2002).

One issue that exists in the selection of a qualified moderator is that the quality and qualifications of moderators now offering their services are quite varied. There are no widely accepted professional requirements for being a qualitative researcher; no special education or experience is demanded.

TABLE 5.2
Personal Traits of Good Qualitative Researchers/Moderators

Good qualitative researchers:

Are genuinely interested in hearing other people's thoughts and feelings	Good moderators are people who in "real life" really are interested in finding out about other questions people ask and listening to the answers. This does not start when someone sits in the moderator's chair.
Are expressive of their own feelings	They not only talk about concrete, objective events but also give their personal reactions.
Are animated and spontaneous	Those with a dull personality will not be able to control focus groups. Spontaneity is vital for a moderator to take advantage of the great many stimuli during a session.
Have a sense of humor	They do not tell canned jokes but find latent humor possibilities in ordinary situations. This quality, more important than it may seem, is strongly related to imagination, creativity, and spontaneity, all needed in qualitative research.
Are empathetic	This ability to understand how others feel and to see life from their perspective is essential.
Admit their own biases	Complete objectivity is impossible, but we can aim for recognition of our own feelings toward the subject with which we are dealing. If qualitative researchers talk about their own experiences or feelings related to a project, clients do not necessarily have to get nervous about their objectivity. The key point is whether we can be honest and introspective enough to understand these biases and professionally detach ourselves from them in our work.

(Continued)

TABLE 5.2 (Continued)

Are insightful about people	True researchers are always exploring, asking why. You do not turn on the psychological probing and turn it off afterward. Good qualitative researchers are truly intrigued with understanding people. This analytical bent shows through in their conversation, whether in personal or professional observations.
Express thoughts clearly	Good moderators must frame questions quickly, and if these cannot be stated simply, the session will not succeed.
Are flexible	They must respond quickly and be able to take new directions before or during sessions. They often face last-minute changes and should be adaptable to recommend changes if a technique is not proving productive enough or if a concept needs revising.

SOURCE: From Langer, J., "Clients: Check Qualitative Researcher's Personal Traits to Get More; Qualitative Researchers: Enter Entire Marketing Process to Give More," *Marketing News,* (Sept. 8), copyright © 1978. Reprinted with permission of the American Marketing Association.

Another factor aggravating the problem of quality control is that there are few special courses or programs designed to improve skills or train researchers in moderating. Much of the "training" of moderators takes place in-house (as in some big research agencies) or is idiosyncratic to a researcher's personal experience and abilities. This makes the task of selecting an appropriate moderator even more difficult because an unqualified moderator may be difficult to identify and can easily undermine the reliability and validity of focus group findings. Awareness of some general personal qualities (as in Table 5.2, for example) and relevant educational background can be a useful starting point in the moderator selection process, however. It is worth noting that what makes an individual a successful researcher or scholar is not necessarily the same thing that makes an individual a good moderator. Many researchers considering the use of focus groups would be well advised to obtain the services of a professional moderator rather than moderate the group themselves.

The effectiveness of a moderator is also determined by situational variables such as sensitivity of the problem, conduciveness of focus group facilities, time constraints, amount of probing required, and the interaction between the demographics (e.g., age, sex, race) of the moderator and those of the focus group participants. There may also be a decision to be made regarding the efficacy of using an older person to moderate a teenage group, a male moderator for distinctively female topics, a culturally incompatible moderator for ethnically sensitive topics, or a novice to moderate highly technical subjects.

Research on the impact of group homogeneity and compatibility on group dynamics, which we reviewed in Chapter 2, seems to suggest that the more compatible the group members (including the moderator), the greater the interaction and the more open the communication. But there is no conclusive evidence that in fairly cosmopolitan or racially integrated cultures, demographic differences between the moderator and the focus group participants will bias the research findings.

In addition to variations in the focus group participants' characteristics and the adequacy of focus group facilities, a moderator frequently encounters constraints or deadlines for conducting focus group interviews. The funds available for research often determine the number and duration of focus group interviews that can be meaningfully conducted. The depth of probing required versus that actually achieved is often a function of the scope of the problem, the number of questions, the sensitivity of the topic, and the comfort levels of the participants. Thus, making allowances for resource constraints is as important as ensuring a proper composition of focus group participants and comfortable focus group surroundings.

With training and experience, moderators can become better aware of these types of situational interactions and their impact on the usefulness and validity of focus group data. Such awareness often encourages or facilitates preplanning on the part of the moderator to develop strategies to overcome problems such as noncooperative or disruptive behaviors that may arise from participants' sensitivities. The unintended consequences of moderator behavior that may bias the integrity of the data may also be mitigated by adequate preparation and planning.

MODERATOR PREPARATION

Moderator preparation should involve both an understanding of the nature of the research problem and the potential nature of the group dynamics that may arise as a result of group composition, the topic to be discussed, and the physical setting of the group. An understanding of group dynamics and leadership emergence may help the moderator anticipate problems and design strategies to moderate the disruptive behavior of emergent leaders among focus group participants. Because most of the time such behaviors are unavoidable, the more productive approach would be to seek the assistance of emergent leaders in generating discussion and increasing enthusiasm among group members. This would be a more viable approach in situations when participants have great respect for a particular group member by virtue of his or her experience or expertise with the topic being discussed. We discuss more specific strategies for dealing with these problems in Chapter 6.

Pregroup preparation of the moderator is a critical factor in the success of a focus group as both a social-interaction and a research tool. Unfortunately, in many commercial focus group settings, moderator preparation is frequently sabotaged by giving the moderator the discussion guide less than an hour prior to the focus group's start time. Providing adequate preparation time and background information for the moderator will pay large dividends in terms of the information obtained from a focus group.

An important aspect of moderator preparation involves learning how to deal with focus groups of different sizes. The size of the focus group may affect the success of moderators. Using the number of ideas generated as a measure of effectiveness, Fern (1982) found that 8-member groups generated significantly more ideas than 4-member groups. There is really no hard and fast rule about the optimal size of the focus group, however. As we noted in Chapter 3, the ideal range seems to be 8 to 12 people. Fewer than 8 respondents may result in the discussion being somewhat narrow and biased in favor of a few individuals in the group. On the other hand, 10 to 12 people may be too many, depending on the composition of the group and the nature of the topic to be discussed. Levy (1979) provided a succinct description of problems associated with increasing group size:

> As the group grows in size, opportunities to address it decline, people have to wait more for their turns, and are frustrated by more views that they have less chance to respond to. They are also more widely dispersed in the room or around the table. The tendency for the group to fragment becomes great, and, as a result, the problems of controlling the conversation are magnified. There are likely to be distractions, frequent murmuring, dissipation of remarks in side conversations, sly antagonisms. The moderator is pressed toward the role of disciplinarian and classroom behavior, cautioning the group to be quiet, asking for a show of hands, questioning individuals in turn to be sure everyone gets a vote. The problems grow without necessarily enlarging the pool of information or range of themes that emerge. (p. 34)

Thus far, the discussion has focused on demographic and behavioral influences of moderator effectiveness. We have noted, however, that preparation on the part of the moderator must also involve understanding the nature and scope of the research problem, prioritizing the different objectives of the research, determining the appropriate depth of probing, being up to date and familiar with the topic or object of discussion, and deciding on the strategy and sequencing of questioning that will facilitate discussion and ultimately the analysis and interpretation of the data. The moderator must also be prepared to (a) deal with premature stagnation of participation by renewing interest and enthusiasm and (b) handle new or unexpected information by adapting the interview guide. A part of the preparation of the moderator should include identification of those points in the interview when interest may lag or when discussion may become very intense. Such preparation provides strategies for moving the group on to new topics or discussion of the same topic at a different level of detail or abstraction.

One major dimension of moderator preparation is developing a good questioning strategy. Our brief review earlier in the chapter highlighted different types of questions and sequences of those questions. The primary purpose of any questioning strategy is to address problems or issues for which the focus group interview was designed. When the objectives of the focus group are clear, moderators can use different kinds of questions to get at different aspects of the topic or problem. Wheatley and Flexner (1988) provide a useful typology of questions and the usage situations to which they apply. This typology is summarized in Table 5.3, and it further elaborates the demanding set of skills that successful moderators require.

There are, however, situations when an *unfocussed* approach may be more appropriate. This is an especially appropriate approach when respondents need to learn about a new concept or category, for idea generation or for separating good ideas from bad. In these circumstances, neither the researcher nor the moderator may know enough about the topic to be able to come up with a detailed list of questions. Sometimes the purpose of the "*un*focus" group is to find out the type of questions to ask, which may then be used for another focus group or for designing a survey instrument. This would be a case when a rolling interview guide, as discussed in Chapter 4, would be appropriate.

Schoenfeld (1988) provides guidelines for using the unfocussed approach to group interviewing:

- Throw away the outline.
- Provide the panelists a wide variety of ideas or stimuli to stimulate them.
- Never call on panelists directly or force a response out of them.
- Warm up panelists—not on the subject or topic—but by practicing disagreement.

Thus, we see that just as leadership styles need to be varied according to the purpose of the research, the composition of the group, and the task situation, moderating style also needs to be adjusted for these same factors. However, certain moderating styles may introduce biases that affect the validity of the focus group research findings. We now turn our attention to some of the sources and nature of moderator-induced biases.

TABLE 5.3
A Typology of Focus Group Questions

Type of Questions	Purpose/Usage Situation
• **Main research questions**	Used to focus discussion on issues directly related to the purpose of the session. Exactly how you are going to ask these questions should be thought out beforehand.
• **Leading questions**	Useful for carrying a discussion toward deeper meaning and are especially useful if the group seems hesitant to pursue it. Formulate the questions using the group's words and ideas and by asking, "Why?"
• **Testing questions**	Used to test the limits of a concept. Use the group's words and ideas to formulate the question, this time feeding the concepts back to participants in a more extreme, yet tentative form, as though you may have misunderstood.
• **Steering questions**	Used to nudge the group back onto the main research questions, following excursions into other areas.
• **Obtuse questions**	Often the discussion will go into territory uncomfortable to the group. To further pursue topics into such areas, you need to back the questions off one level of abstraction, allowing the group to discuss other people's reactions or opinions, not necessarily their own: "Why do you suppose someone would feel this way?"
• **Factual questions**	Useful for neutralizing emotionally charged groups or discussions, these questions have a factual answer and permit the group to answer without personal risk.
• **"Feel" questions**	Used to ask for opinions surrounded by personal feelings. Feel questions ask participants to take risks and expose their personal feelings. They are the most dangerous and most fertile of question types.
	The rule to remember here is that every person is entitled to his or her feelings, and no one else can disagree with or discount them, though many will try.

Type of Questions	Purpose/Usage Situation
• **Anonymous questions**	Used to get a group talking, comfortable with each other, or refocused on a key question. They generally take the form, "Please take the index card in front of you and write down the single idea that comes to mind regarding this issue."
• **Silence**	Often the best question is no question. Many group leaders tend to fill in every void in the discussion. Simply waiting for a response allows those who are a little slower or uncertain to formulate their ideas.

SOURCE: From Langer, J., "Clients: Check Qualitative Researcher's Personal Traits to Get More; Qualitative Researchers: Enter Entire Marketing Process to Give More," *Marketing News,* (Sept. 8), copyright © 1978. Reprinted with permission of the American Marketing Association.

MODERATOR BIAS IN FOCUS GROUP INTERVIEWS

Two important aspects of moderator preparation are developing (a) an understanding of the sources and nature of biases that can affect the validity of the focus group data and (b) an understanding of the steps that might be taken to cope with these biases. Moderator bias can be introduced both intentionally and unintentionally. Kennedy (1976, p. 19) highlights three different sources of bias that threaten moderator objectivity:

- *Personal bias.* The all-too-human predisposition to welcome and reinforce the expression of points of view that are consonant with our own
- *Unconscious needs to "please" the client.* The predisposition to welcome and reinforce the expression of points of view that are consonant with those of our clients, those for whom we are doing the research
- *The need for consistency.* The predisposition to welcome and reinforce the expression of points of view that are internally consistent

The following are examples of how these different sources of bias are manifested in practice (Kennedy, 1976):

Most often, by greeting favorable comments with appreciative nods, smiles or reinforcing comments, and by responding to unfavorable comments with indifference, perplexed stares, or body movements that reflect discomfort.

By being patient, permissive and encouraging when someone finds it difficult to articulate a favorable thought, but by providing no such assistance to one who finds it difficult to express an unfavorable position.

By initiating a round of questioning with a favorably inclined respondent, so that a favorable view will set a precedent and context for subsequent inquiries.

By failing to probe for contrary sentiments when favorable comments are expressed, but by probing actively when unfavorable comments are articulated.

By more actively directing questions to those who seem most likely to hold favorable views, and by ignoring those who seem most likely to hold unfavorable views.

By "turning on the charm" so that respondents will tend to go along with the position you have unconsciously conveyed you want to hear.

By permitting "out of context" favorable comments, while telling those who offer an unfavorable view out of context that "we'll talk about that later."

In periodic summaries of group positions, understating or omitting "minority" points of view. (p. 21)

Possessing the appropriate training and experience does not guarantee a bias-free focus group session. The researcher and research sponsor need to take an active role to understand the pressures being applied on the moderator and work closely with him or her—during both the preparation and the postinterview phases—to avoid biasing the outcome of a group.

CONCLUSION

In this chapter, we have reviewed a variety of issues related to the training, preparation, and selection of focus group moderators. We have considered the importance of leadership style, approaches to questioning of respondents, and moderator characteristics and behaviors that may bias the results of a focus group. An important aspect of moderator training and preparation involves learning how to deal with situational variables such as disruptive focus group participants, emergent leaders, different focus group sizes, deadlines, and other resource constraints. Personal characteristics, educational background and training, and amount of moderating experiences are important considerations in selecting a moderator. However, we have suggested that there is no one best style for leading a focus group, nor is there a single best "type" of moderator. Rather, both the moderator and the strategy for conducting the interview must be matched with the purpose of the research and the characteristics of the group.

REVIEW QUESTIONS

1. Is there such a thing as an ideal or best moderator? Discuss.
2. How can an understanding of leadership qualities and behaviors improve our ability to select good moderators?

3. Compare and contrast effective leaders and effective moderators.

4. How can personal characteristics (e.g., age, sex, personality) and physical appearance of the moderator influence his or her ability to moderate effectively?

5. Knowing what questions to ask and when to ask them is an important quality that a good moderator should possess. Discuss the various types of questions and the situations for which they are appropriate.

6. An important aspect of interviewing style is the sequence in which questions are asked. For sensitive topics (e.g., racially sensitive topics), what approach would be most appropriate? Are there situations when the sequencing strategy really does not matter?

7. Indicate, briefly, how situational variables such as the physical setting, time constraints, or the seating arrangement can influence the effectiveness of a moderator?

8. Moderator preparation involves more than just having a good understanding of the nature and scope of the research problem. What are some of the procedural and behavioral problems that a moderator needs to anticipate and prepare for before actually conducting the focus group?

9. The validity of focus group findings can be easily compromised by the presence of moderator bias. Bias may be introduced either intentionally or unintentionally. What are some of the sources of moderator bias? Discuss their implications for focus group findings.

Exercise: What type of moderator would be most appropriate for leading focus group discussions of each of the topics below? Why?

a. The use of condoms among males from lower socioeconomic groups

b. The desirability of a value-added tax to support public schools

c. The value of a new operating system for personal computers

d. Interest in a new "convenience-baking" product

e. Reasons for shoplifting among a group of convicted shoplifters

6

Conducting the Focus Group

In the previous chapter, we discussed the role of the moderator and some general strategies for conducting focus groups. These strategies include the leadership style, degree of structure, and sequencing of questions that are most appropriate for a given research situation. The focus group research situation is itself a complex interaction of the purpose of the research, the composition of the group, and the physical setting in which the group takes place. Earlier in the book, we discussed how these individual factors may influence the character of a focus group discussion. We have not yet discussed the actual conduct of a focus group, nor have we offered strategies for coping with specific opportunities or problems that may arise in the course of an interview. The purpose of this chapter is to consider issues related to the actual conduct of a focus group interview.

Focus group sessions are usually stimulating and fun for participants, observers, and the moderator. We noted in Chapter 4 that having fun helps the flow of discussion and builds a sense of trust among members of the group. It must be recognized, however, that the primary purpose of a focus group is to obtain information. In the previous chapter, we emphasized the importance of ensuring that the group discussion stays on the topic of interest. It is the primary responsibility of the moderator to keep the group focused on the relevant topics and to ensure that the session yields useful information. As we have seen, the role of moderator requires training, experience, and a special blend of personality characteristics.

The initial job of the interviewer is to create a nonthreatening and nonevaluative environment in which group members feel free to express themselves openly and without concern for whether others in the group agree with the opinions offered. Once this environment has been established, it is the job of the moderator to keep the discussion on track, manage the time, and ensure the active participation of all members of the group. Moderating a focus group is hard work, and it requires that the moderator be constantly alert. Every group takes on a unique identity, and no two groups behave the same way, even when discussing the same topic with the same questions. There are, however, issues and problems common to all focus group discussions.

THE PHYSICAL ARRANGEMENT OF THE GROUP

In Chapter 3, we suggested that a focus group may be held in a variety of settings. We qualified this suggestion in Chapter 4, where we noted that the physical environment of the group can influence the nature of the interaction among group members and the types and amount of information obtained. In these earlier discussions, we noted the physical arrangement of the group within a given setting is especially critical to the success of the group discussion. Because the object of a focus group is discussion, the group members should be seated in a manner that provides maximum opportunity for eye contact with both the moderator and other group members. When a circular arrangement or reasonable approximation is not possible, Krueger and Casey (2000) suggest placing the least talkative individuals directly across from the moderator and the most talkative respondents and experts to the sides of the interviewer. This tends to increase the frequency of comments of the least talkative individuals and reduce the frequency of comments by the most talkative participants, providing greater balance for the discussion. On the other hand, it may be difficult to determine in advance how talkative different participants might be.

Most participants in focus groups feel more comfortable when seated around a table. There are a number of reasons for this. A table provides something of a protective barrier between respondents that gives less secure or more reserved members of the group a sense of security. It also helps establish a sense of territoriality and personal space that makes participants more comfortable. In groups consisting of both men and women, a table provides a shield for the legs, eliminating a source of distraction. Finally, a table provides a place for resting one's arms and hands and when food is served, may eliminate gymnastics associated with handling plates and cups in one's lap.

Some moderators prefer that each member of the group have a name tag. To ensure some protection of the privacy of the participants, only first names should be used. The availability of names provides a basis for building greater rapport among group members. At a minimum, the moderator should have a list of first names corresponding to the seating arrangement of the participants. This allows the interviewer to direct questions at group members by name with immediate and simultaneous eye contact. It also creates a greater sense of group identity and cohesiveness.

INTERVIEWING STYLE

As we noted in Chapter 5, moderators of focus groups may use a wide variety of styles. Interviewing styles vary because of personality differences among moderators and because different types of groups and different research questions require different approaches. As we have already noted, one important dimension along which interviewing styles may vary is the degree of control or directiveness that the interviewer uses. Interviewing styles may range from extremely directive to very nondirective. At the extreme of the directive style is the nominal group. In the *nominal group,* there is only an interchange between the moderator and individual members of the group; little or no interchange among members of the group is permitted, and the interviewer exercises tight control over the agenda for discussion. At the other extreme, the moderator participates only at the start of the discussion and interjects him- or herself only when it is necessary to keep the discussion on the topic of interest. Both approaches have advantages and disadvantages.

The *directive* approach generally allows for greater coverage of topics or more detailed coverage of specific topics of interest in the time available but at the cost of group synergy and spontaneity. *Nondirective* approaches provide more opportunity for group interaction and discovery and greater opportunity for the individual participants' views to emerge, rather than the researcher framing of the issues imposed on them. Although this risks less coverage of the key research topics, it has the advantage of providing a validity check on the researcher's understanding of the problem and its relevant dimensions.

Most focus group discussions involve an interviewing style somewhere between the two extremes. A certain amount of direction and structure is useful for moving the discussion along, for controlling dominant group members, and for drawing out reticent respondents. Still, interviewing styles will vary in terms of directiveness, and it is useful for the moderator to have a clear understanding of the level of directiveness that is desirable for the research question and group of respondents. Because focus group discussions tend to move along spontaneously and because the interaction of participants within individual groups tends to differ, the ideal moderator is one who is comfortable using different styles of interviewing, ranging from nondirective to directive. As we noted in the previous chapter, however, there will be cases when it may be necessary to select a moderator with a given interviewing style because not all moderators can easily move from a directive to a nondirective style as needed. This requires knowledge of the particular strengths and weaknesses of a moderator. This is one reason it is important either to have direct experience with potential moderators or to carefully check their references. Selection of a moderator is not just a matter of competence but competence for a particular type of task. Questioning potential moderators and their references with respect to interviewing style is an important element in the design of focus group research.

DISCUSSION AIDS

Interviewing style may also vary with respect to the use of discussion aids. Some interviews can be carried out with the moderator simply raising questions. In other cases, the discussion may be facilitated and enriched by presentations or demonstrations. In marketing research applications of focus groups, it is often useful to have respondents sample a product or watch the product in use as a means for stimulating discussion. Merton's early use of "focussed" interviews had respondents focus on positive and negative responses they had recorded at various points in a radio program. Focus groups used to evaluate advertising or training programs often expose group members to the ad or program prior to the beginning of the discussion.

In addition to demonstrating or displaying the object for discussion, the interviewer may use a variety of other discussion aids. Projective techniques are often useful discussion aids, particularly when group members are reluctant to talk about an issue or the issue may involve deeply rooted values or feelings that respondents have difficulty identifying or articulating. Word association techniques and sentence completion tasks can be very useful for provoking discussion and are usually found to be very entertaining by many group members. Zaltman (2003) developed an elicitation technique that encourages respondents to identify pictures in magazines that represent their feelings and opinions. Responses to such association completion and picture identification tasks can be followed with additional questions to try to uncover reasons for a particular response.

Storytelling is another useful discussion aid. The interviewer may ask respondents to tell a story about a particular incident involving the object of the research. One way to facilitate storytelling is with pictures or cartoons. Respondents may be shown a picture of a situation, product, object, or person and asked to tell a story. Advertising and marketing researchers will occasionally use a set of pictures of people of various types and ask group members to identify the type of person who uses a particular product. Follow-up questions are then used to determine why a given person was selected. Sayre (2001) and Mariampolski (2001) provide extensive discussions of the uses of projective methods in both individual and group interviews.

INTIMACY

A third dimension along which interviewing style may vary is the level of intimacy on the part of the interviewer. In some cases, the interviewer takes an objective, distanced stance with respect to the group. In other cases, the interviewer may facilitate discussion by offering personal anecdotes and examples. In discussions of very sensitive topics, the more intimate approach may serve to relax respondents and stimulate discussion. For example, a moderator might use a personal situation relevant to the topic at hand or tell a personal story related to the topic as a way of helping group members overcome their embarrassment or sensitivity. By offering personal information that is potentially embarrassing, the moderator legitimizes such information and provides an example for others. The danger of the more intimate approach is that the more the moderator becomes a participating member of the group, the more the group will provide the types of responses they think the interviewer wants. Use of an intimate interviewing style without biasing responses of the group is a difficult task, even for an experienced moderator.

OBSERVERS AND RECORDINGS

It is very common for focus groups to be observed by others and for sessions to be recorded on either audio- or videotape. There is seldom reason to believe that observation or taping radically alters responses of members in a focus group. The group setting already makes all comments public. Nevertheless, there are some courtesies and precautions that are warranted.

It is customary to inform group members at the outset of the session that observers are present and audio or video recording is taking place. Generally, group members are required to give their permission for videotaping and many institutional review boards require written consent. If observers are behind a one-way mirror, it is sufficient to simply tell the group that observers are present. When the observers are in the same room with the group, they should be seated away from the group as a reminder (to them and to the group) that they are observers, not participants. An introduction of the observers, by name only, is appropriate in this latter situation, along with an explanation that they are there to observe. It is usually not a good idea to identify the organization or title of the observers or the reason they are observing. Such identifying information, when provided at the beginning of a session, may reveal too much too soon about the nature of the interview and may bias responses of the participants. On the other hand, the end of the group discussion is sometimes a good opportunity to let the participants know why, and perhaps for whom, the research is being carried out. Debriefing participants at the end of a session is a matter of courtesy, though the amount of information revealed will vary by topic and security conditions. For example, a manufacturer contemplating a new product might not wish to reveal its plans but might tell participants that it is exploring opportunities for new product development.

There are occasions when this debriefing exercise may be a stimulus for further discussion, which may provide useful insights. For example, in a focus group conducted by one of the authors, revealing the identity of the sponsor of the group unleashed a stream of complaints that had not yet surfaced. Because the purpose of the group was to identify sources of dissatisfaction, the debriefing exercise provided information that was particularly helpful.

When recording equipment is used, it is customary to acknowledge its presence while assuring group members that the recording will remain confidential and its circulation will be limited. The moderator might suggest that the recordings replace notes and facilitate report writing. Group members who are uncomfortable with being recorded should be given the opportunity to leave the session without embarrassment.

Although the presence of observers or the use of recording equipment may make some group members self-conscious, at least initially, the stimulation and excitement of discussion generally causes the respondents to forget their presence. It is usually not a good idea for the moderator to remind group members of the presence of recording equipment by exhorting them to speak up, however. It is just as easy to ask a participant to speak up so that others in the group can hear or so that the moderator can hear.

The presence of observers is very useful as a tool for expanding the impact and salience of information obtained from a focus group. An observer's hearing respondents' comments directly is far more compelling than the summary provided by a moderator after the group is over (see Barabba, 1995, for a useful discussion of the power of direct observation). However, it is important that observers know their role and not become a source of distraction, especially when the observers are actually in the room. A quick route to a silent group is to have group members hear laughter coming from behind the observation window. One way to ensure that observers understand their role is to give each observer a specific set of responsibilities. If only one observer is present, this might involve detailed note taking. If multiple observers are present, each can be assigned responsibility for taking notes about one or more of the participants, including not only what the participants say but also their behavior, gestures, and other types of nonverbal responses.

BEGINNING THE INTERVIEW

The beginning of an interview sets the tone and agenda for all that comes later. The moderator should attempt to create an atmosphere of trust and openness at the very beginning. Reassurances of anonymity, of the value of all opinions, regardless of how different or unusual, and of empathy for the respondents are very important. The moderator should establish the agenda for the discussion and outline the ground rules for the session. Such agenda setting may be more or less directive, depending on the purpose of the group and the style of the moderator, but it will generally include some opportunity for respondents to introduce themselves. Typical openings might take the following form:

> Before we begin our discussion, it will be helpful for us to get acquainted with one another. Let's begin with some introductory comments about ourselves. X, why don't you start, and we'll go around the table, give our first names, and say a little about how we like to spend our leisure time.
>
> Today we're going to discuss an issue that affects all of you. Before we get into our discussion, let me make a few requests of you. First, you should know that we are videotaping the session so that I can refer back to the discussion when I write my report. If anyone is uncomfortable with being recorded please say so, and of course you are free to leave. Do speak up, and let's try to have just one person speak at a time. I will play traffic cop and try to ensure that everyone gets a turn. Finally, please say exactly what you think. Don't worry about what you think I think or what your neighbor thinks. We're here to exchange opinions and have some fun while we do it. Why don't we begin by introducing ourselves.

Introductions of group members are a good way to build rapport and a sense of group. It is always a good idea to have group members introduce themselves and tell a little about themselves, such as their work, their families, or other nonintimate personal facts. In some groups, the moderator may want to limit the types of personal information group members provide. For example, in a group of experts and novices on a topic, identification of occupation may serve to intimidate novices or give undue weight to the experts' opinions. There are no hard and fast rules with respect to the amount of information participants should be allowed to reveal about themselves, but if there is good reason to believe that such information might bias the group or otherwise influence the nature of the group's interaction, it would be wise for the moderator to ask the group not to mention it.

Once introductions are finished, the moderator should introduce the topic for discussion. Most often the moderator will introduce the topic in its most general form and leave more specific questions and issues for later questioning. This serves the useful function of getting the topic on the table without revealing all the specific issues that are of interest. Of course, this is a funnel approach to interviewing, which we discussed in Chapter 5. We also introduced several other approaches to interviewing in Chapter 5, and there are situations when other interviewing formats—and hence introductions to the topic for discussion—will be more appropriate. Nevertheless, the funnel approach tends to be the most commonly used. One reason for this is that it is often useful to know whether an issue is important enough for participants to raise it on their own. In addition, very specific questions about the topic, if asked too early, may set the discussion on a track that is too focused and narrow. Rather, it is better to funnel the discussion as it progresses by moving from the general to the specific. One way to engage the interest of participants quickly is to raise the topic for discussion and ask for personal anecdotes related to the topic. The sharing of stories tends to further build rapport and break down inhibitions.

ENSURING PARTICIPATION

Members of a focus group should be made to feel that their presence and opinions are not only valued but necessary for the success of the group. It is particularly important to establish this at the beginning of the interview. This will reassure the reticent, less forward respondents and provide a basis for dealing with dominant members of the group if it proves necessary. During the session, all members of the group should be encouraged to speak. This can be accomplished by asking direct questions of a member of the group. The simplest technique to ensure participation is to ask each group member for his or her opinion in turn. This procedure cannot be used with each question because it tends to stifle interaction among the group members, but it can be used several times during the group to draw out reluctant respondents. Within the context of focus group research, such a "polling" procedure is appropriate only as a device for facilitating discussion. As noted elsewhere in this book, focus groups are inappropriate for "surveying" respondents to generate percentages or other statistics.

The moderator needs to be particularly sensitive to the nonverbal cues used by group members. Facial expressions and gestures often suggest occasions when an individual is about to speak, disagrees, is puzzled by something that has been said, or requires reassurance that an expressed opinion is accepted. We have noted in previous chapters that the moderator's ability to recognize and respond to these cues can dramatically increase the balance of participation within the group.

TIME MANAGEMENT

One of the most important skills of the moderator is time management. The moderator must gauge the extent to which a topic has been exhausted and further discussion will yield little new information. Knowledge of the relative importance of various specific questions to the research agenda is also helpful because it provides some guidance with respect to the amount of time that should be devoted to each question and which ones might be eliminated if time runs short. One critical point to bear in mind is that the participants have been recruited for a specific length of time. There is an implicit contract with the group that it will be finished on schedule. Groups that are kept beyond the appointed hour have been known to become surly and hostile.

The beginning of the interview is often the most difficult to manage. Discussions usually develop a large range of ideas quickly. The moderator must try to record these ideas mentally or on paper so that they can all be dealt with in turn, if appropriate. Only one issue can be discussed at a time, and the moderator must keep the group on this one topic until discussion has been exhausted. This may involve telling group members that a particularly interesting but not immediately relevant issue will be dealt with later. Another way to manage the discussion is to use a flip chart on which topics introduced at the beginning of the group discussion are recorded. This written record can then be used for directing the group from topic to topic.

PROBING

Participants in focus groups do not always say everything they wish, nor do they necessarily readily articulate what they think. Sometimes participants will signal that they have more to say by using nonverbal cues such as stopping in midsentence, continuing to look at the moderator after finishing a statement, or through facial expressions. The moderator needs to recognize these cues and follow them up with acknowledgment and encouragement to continue speaking. In other cases, it may simply be unclear what the respondent meant. This too requires follow-up questioning.

The first response of a group participant is often incomplete. Initial responses are often glib and involve abstract shorthand terms that are not very meaningful. For example, a respondent who suggests his or her health care provider is unfriendly is likely responding to something very specific. It may be that the provider does not smile much, or it could be that the provider is hard to contact by telephone. Similarly, a consumer who indicates that a product is cheap or low in quality is most likely responding to some very specific characteristic of the product. It is very important to ask probing follow-up questions to identify the specific meaning of the group participants.

Follow-up questions, or *probes,* are an important part of extracting full information from respondents. Probes can take a variety of forms. They may simply acknowledge that a given participant has not given up the floor. This may involve continued eye contact with the participant and a simple "uh-huh," or it might involve telling the next person that speaks that X doesn't seem to have finished his or her thought. Another type of probe involves reflecting the respondents' thoughts back to him or her: "What I heard you say was. . . ."

The moderator may also ask for more information by saying "Tell me more" or "I don't quite understand. Can you explain what you mean?" Asking for an illustration, an example, or a story is another way of obtaining further information. Other probes may be directed at the group at large. The group might be asked, "Does anyone have an example of that?" or "Is this anyone else's experience?" It is generally not a good idea to probe by directly asking if anyone agrees or disagrees with the preceding statement. This results in a defensive respondent and sets the stage for conflict. Rather, the moderator might ask, "Does anyone have a similar (different) perspective?"

In some cases, the moderator may wish to enlist the entire group in aiding one respondent's explanation. This may be accomplished if the moderator plays dumb and asks, "You all seem to understand what she is saying, but I'm still confused. Can anyone help me?"

There are some things that just cannot be easily articulated. Probes in such cases may need to take the form of requests for demonstration ("Can you show me?") or the use of analogy ("Tell me what it is like"). Finally, a good moderator will allow other group members to do the probing for him or her when possible. If someone looks puzzled at a comment by another group member, the moderator might ask, "You look puzzled. Why? What don't you understand?"

Probes are a critical part of extracting information in focus groups. Good probes ask for more information without suggesting a specific answer and without making the respondent defensive. Knowing when to probe and when further probing is unlikely to be helpful is also critical to successfully managing the agenda for the discussion within the allotted time.

PROBLEMS

Problems can take a variety of forms in a focus group interview. It is impossible to identify or anticipate all of the problems that might come up during a session. Participants spill coffee, become ill, and receive emergency telephone calls. Cellular telephones have become so ubiquitous that the moderator should ask that they be turned off at the beginning of the session. The moderator must be prepared for anything that may happen and swiftly move the group back to its task if possible. Although it is not possible to anticipate all problems, several occur with sufficient frequency that they require some discussion.

Experts

Two types of experts may be found in focus groups: legitimate experts and self-appointed experts (Krueger & Casey, 2000). Although there may be many occasions when a focus group composed exclusively of experts is useful, the presence of a legitimate expert among a group of novices may inhibit the discussion. Screening during the recruitment phase of the project may be the most effective means for eliminating this type of problem, but even the most rigorous screening will not prevent an occasional mistake. When such experts do appear in a group, it may be possible to co-opt them by making use of their expertise. This would involve asking the expert to withhold his or her opinions while at the same time occasionally requesting that the expert elaborate on matters of fact or provide detailed descriptive information. This approach often works well because the moderator is seldom as knowledgeable as the legitimate expert, who is placed in an important but clearly delineated role within the group. Use of this technique requires that the moderator not lose control of the group to the expert but use the expert as a resource to facilitate the group discussion.

Self-appointed experts are a more difficult problem for the focus group moderator. Such "experts" seldom have genuine expertise but offer their opinions as fact and often become dominant talkers in the group. These individuals may intimidate other members of the group, yet they cannot be placed so easily into a helpful role as the genuine expert. Nevertheless, it may be possible to control these individuals through a variety of means. The moderator's making it clear that he or she is interested in the views of all members of the group may be sufficient for solving problems created by the self-appointed expert. If this fails, however, the moderator may use more assertive techniques such as cutting the individual off in midsentence, avoiding eye contact, and not recognizing the individual when he or she wishes to speak. Nonverbal cues such as the moderator's looking bored or fatigued; drumming one's fingers; pretending to have a headache; or studying the ceiling, the floor, or anything other than the "expert" may provide a means for muting such individuals. Acting uninterested and immediately changing the subject after the expert speaks may also be useful for maintaining control of the group.

Friends

We have suggested in previous chapters that it is generally unwise to have friends participate in the same group unless the group is specifically designed to bring together individuals who are known to one another. Careful screening during the recruiting phase may reduce the frequency of this occurrence, but it is inevitable that friends will arrive together on occasion. In such cases, it is often appropriate to politely ask one of the individuals to leave.

Templeton (1994) identified a number of problems created by having friends in the same group: friends discourage anonymity; they impair group formation by not joining; they may engage in private conversations that deny their insights to the larger group and inhibit the expression of opinion by others; and friends may endorse one another's views, creating an imbalance of opinion in the group. There may be occasions when having friends (or spouses, other relatives, or persons known to one another) is perfectly consistent with the objectives of the research, but this should be determined at the outset of the research planning process.

Hostile Group Members

It occasionally happens that a person who is clearly hostile will arrive for a focus group session. This individual may simply have had a bad day, or the topic for discussion is not what he or she thought. There are also persons with genuinely hostile personalities who sometimes find their way into a focus group. The presence of such individuals in the group makes everyone uncomfortable and stifles discussion. If hostility is detected prior to the commencement of the group, it would be wise to politely ask the individual if he or she would like to leave. If the hostility emerges during the group discussion, it might be helpful to invite the group to take a short break during which the individual may be invited to leave. If the individual does not wish to leave, then a lack of eye contact may discourage participation without directly evoking further hostility.

SPECIAL ISSUES

One of the advantages of focus group interviewing is that it can be adapted for almost any purpose. Such versatility means, however, that there are numerous issues and problems that may come up in the conduct of focus groups that are specific to a particular application. Researchers who are contemplating using focus groups for a specific purpose would do well to carefully think through the procedure and any problems that might be anticipated. In the remainder of this chapter, we deal with five special issues:

1. The use of children in focus groups
2. The use of observational techniques
3. The discussion of potentially sensitive or embarrassing topics

4. The use of focus groups in international settings
5. The use of virtual focus groups, that is, groups brought together via technology instead of gathered in the same room

Children as Focus Group Participants

Children can make outstanding participants in a focus group, but they pose special problems. The moderator is especially important in ensuring the children are comfortable and relaxed. Children generally know when an adult is uncomfortable with them and this in turn makes them uncomfortable or hostile. Uncomfortable and hostile children do not talk much. Not all moderators, even very good ones, are well suited to the task of interviewing children. It is important then that the moderator be comfortable and experienced with children.

Young children especially are often more comfortable with a female moderator, though depending on the topic and whether the group is mixed or of a single gender, a male or female moderator may be appropriate. Generally, groups of girls will be more comfortable with a female interviewer. Groups of boys may be comfortable with a female interviewer but feel more open to talk about certain topics with a male moderator.

Younger children have less verbal facility than older children and adults so that the use of more stimulus materials may be warranted. Children respond well to pictures and to role playing activities that let them act out their responses. Making questions into a game adds a sense of fun and holds attention better. Younger children have especially short attention spans so the interview will need to be abbreviated or divided into parts.

Children and adolescents also change quickly as they develop and don't mix well with those older or younger. Restricting the age range of participants in any particular group is likely to increase the cohesion of the group and facilitate the discussion. Questions also need to be worded in a way that is appropriate to the age of the participants and should address topics that are age appropriate. Finally, in most cases it will be necessary to obtain permission from parents, school authorities, or others as part of the recruiting process. More extended discussions of the unique issues associated with interviewing children can be found in Vaughn, Schumm, and Singagub (1996) and Krueger and Casey (2000).

Observational Techniques

Regardless of the composition of a focus group, it may be useful to record behavioral data as well as verbal responses. Recording of behavioral data poses special problems. The moderator is too busy running the group to record behavioral data, so one or more observers or recording equipment will be required.

When recording equipment (video cameras or film) is used, it is important to recognize that it records only a limited amount of all behavior. Even when multiple cameras are employed, which can be expensive, their angle and placement will restrict what can be recorded. In addition, they will typically be used to capture multiple respondents' behavior so that close-ups of individual respondents' facial expressions may be difficult to capture. Capturing behavior on film or videotape is only the first step in using behavioral data, however. It will ultimately have to be coded for content and analyzed. When observers are used, coding systems for behavior must be developed in advance so that coders know what to record and how to record it. Whether coding is done live or from tape, it is a good idea to use multiple observers to ensure reliability of the observations.

One technique for examining focus group behavior in response to a particular stimulus object is to have the moderator called out of the room for a few minutes. This allows respondents to talk freely and to interact with the object without the inhibiting presence of the moderator.

Dealing With Sensitive and Embarrassing Topics

Many focus groups deal with topics that are at least potentially sensitive and embarrassing. These topics may range from hemorrhoids to feminine hygiene products to the use of condoms. When dealing with such topics, it is useful for the moderator to let the group know that he or she knows the topic is a sensitive one that people are generally reluctant to talk about. This may be used to lead into a discussion of why this is so, rather than an immediate discussion of the topic itself, allowing participants to become comfortable with the topic. The moderator may also need to spend more time talking about why it is important for the participants to share their insights on the topic and express appreciation for the willingness of the respondents to be involved in the discussion.

The comfort level of participants may also be increased if the moderator uses a more intimate approach when appropriate. For example, the moderator might offer a personal anecdote such as, "The first time I ever saw a condom. . . ." Another approach is to invite participants to discuss experiences or views of their acquaintances, friends, or neighbors. This eliminates some potential for personal embarrassment. Beginning a discussion by focusing on friends and acquaintances also helps create an atmosphere conducive to sharing personal experiences later in the discussion. More generally, projective techniques are often useful in eliciting data about sensitive topics, and they often inject humor into the group, which further reduces participants' resistance.

The moderator may also need to take a firm hand when a group member attempts to make light of the topic or embarrass another group member. On the other hand, it is important to recognize that humor is a very useful device for diffusing anxiety. A harmless comment or joke may serve to break the ice and let everyone know that it is OK to have a little fun with the topic, even when it is at one's own expense. A skillful moderator will use humor to best advantage in such situations while still being sensitive to the need to protect individual group members from unfair attempts at humor.

Focus Groups in International Settings

Focus groups are used around the world. Just as culture influences other types of human behavior and social interaction so too does it influence participation in focus groups. Many of the approaches that work in one country do not translate well to another. Serving food is often appropriate but may have a more facilitating effect in cultures like the United States and Japan where "grazing" is common rather than in cultures where longer sit-down meals are the custom. Similarly, some cultures are more accepting of status differences among group members. In hierarchical cultures where status is especially important (e.g., Thailand), groups will need to be more homogeneous with respect to status and power differences. Groups may work better for some topics in some cultures when the ethnicity of respondents is similar. This is especially true if there are very large differences in the behavior or issues on which the group focuses.

It is almost always best to conduct a focus group in the local language of participants. In some cases, there may be a common language that can be used by all participants, but this inevitably reduces the ability of respondents to articulate their opinions. Moderators should speak the language in which the group is conducted as a first language. Even the most fluent person in a second language will have some difficulty framing questions and following up responses. Interpreters create even greater problems and should be avoided whenever possible. It is often the case that the perceptions and opinions of the interpreter color the translation.

Other cultural differences that need to be considered are related to cultural differences about the importance of time. In some cultures, there will be a strong expectation that groups will start and end promptly at the scheduled times. Other cultures are more casual about time, and it may be necessary to plan to start a group discussion well after the scheduled start time. Depending on history and the current political environment, there may be a need to be especially reassuring with respect to the confidentiality of participants' opinions. Concerns for confidentiality, as well as general cultural norms related to audio or video recording, may also limit the ability to make permanent recordings of the group discussion. See Stewart and Shamdasani (1992) for further discussion of issues related to the conduct of focus groups in international settings.

Virtual Focus Groups

Technology has made it possible to link people who are scattered across very broad geographic regions, allowing interviews with highly specialized groups that might be difficult to assemble in a single location. The potential anonymity of virtual groups may also improve participants' willingness when the topic is sensitive or potentially embarrassing. This latter advantage needs to be weighed against the prospect that group participants may not be who they represent themselves to be and the concern of some potential participants about sharing personal information with strangers in an electronic context.

Use of virtual groups greatly expands the pool of potential participants and adds considerable flexibility to the process of scheduling an interview. Busy professionals and executives who might otherwise be unavailable for a face-to-face meeting can often be reached by means of information technologies. Virtual focus groups may be the only option for certain types of samples, but they are not without some costs relative to more traditional groups. The lack of face-to-face interaction often reduces the spontaneity of the group and eliminates the nonverbal communication that plays a key role in eliciting responses. Such nonverbal communication is often critical for determining when further questioning or probing will be useful and is often an important source of interplay among group members. Use of virtual groups tends to reduce the intimacy of the group as well, making group members less likely to be open and spontaneous.

In virtual groups, the moderator's role is made more difficult because it is harder to control the participants. Dominant participants are more difficult to quiet, and less active participants are more difficult to recognize. On the other hand, the moderator's task can be aided by electronic monitoring equipment that keeps an ongoing record of who has talked and for how long. A visual display can keep the names and frequency of participation of group members before the moderator. Thus, the moderator can draw out the quiet participants, just as in a more typical focus group.

Virtual groups can take several forms. Telephonic groups (essentially conference calls) have long been used by researchers, but such groups are very awkward, and it is difficult to manage any serious group interaction. Spontaneity is highly constrained in such groups. Real-time videoconferences have become a common means for conducting virtual groups in the last several years.

Videoconferencing via telephone lines or the Internet can provide an opportunity for the moderator to see participants and for participants to see the moderator and other participants. The success of such groups critically depends on the reliability of the technology. It is always important that technical support be available during the session.

Many research firms that specialize in focus group research now include virtual group capabilities as part of their facility offerings. Virtual groups conducted by videoconference are not a perfect substitute for on-site groups. The facial expressions and other behavior of group members may not be visible at all or may not be as visible as in face-to-face group encounters. Group interaction tends to be less spontaneous. Such groups are inevitably more expensive than more traditional on-site groups because of the cost of the technology, the need for a technician, and the cost of connect time.

Two other alternatives for conducting virtual groups involve the use of chat rooms, blogs, bulletin boards, and similar Web-based sites. Chat rooms involve real-time interaction among the moderator and group members. Bulletin boards are asynchronous, so questions can be posed and answers provided over some extended period of time. Blogs provide individual opinions and often elicit responses from others. Such virtual groups can be very real social groups, but many people remain uncomfortable with such online sharing. It is also the case that the moderator and participants cannot see one another, so information that might be present in facial expressions, tone of voice, and other nonverbal behavior is lost. These alternatives involve creating such sites for research purposes and require the same care and planning as any research project. An important element of the success of such alternatives is that respondents have the opportunity to interact with one another and to build on prior responses of group members. Observation of naturally occurring chat rooms, bulletin boards, and other online sites may reveal interesting information, but they are not substitutes for carefully designed research.

CONCLUSION

Conducting a focus group is an art that requires considerable experience and training. The quality of the data obtained from a focus group discussion is the direct result of how well the moderator carries out the interview. This begins by establishing a high level of comfort for participants in an atmosphere that is perceived as nonevaluative and nonthreatening. In this setting, the moderator moves the group from topic to topic, probing as needed to extract the respondents' meanings. At the same time, the moderator must maintain control of the group, ensuring that the group is not dominated by one member and that all members actively contribute to the discussion.

The moderator must establish the ground rules for the discussion at the outset of the meeting. The moderator must also ensure that all members of the group have an opportunity to contribute to the discussion. This may require co-opting some members of the group or using negative sanctions to control the behavior of particularly assertive members of the group.

The moderator must determine the appropriate level of directiveness, structure, intimacy, and use of discussion aids. These levels should be consistent with the purposes of the research. The use of recording equipment, such as tape recorders and video cameras, must also be explained to participants, as well as the presence of any observers of the group. Finally, the moderator has an obligation to debrief participants about the purposes of the group discussion.

REVIEW QUESTIONS

1. What is the best physical arrangement for a focus group discussion? Why? Would there be occasions where a different arrangement might be optimal?

2. How do directive and nondirective interviewing styles differ? What are the advantages and disadvantages of each style?

3. What types of discussion aids might be used in a focus group? Why are these useful?

4. What is meant by the level of intimacy on the part of the interviewer? How is intimacy related to the quality of the data obtained in a focus group?

5. What factors and issues must be considered when using observers and making recordings in focus group sessions?

6. Why is the beginning of the focus group interview so critical? What are the components of a good beginning?

7. How can the moderator of a focus group ensure that all members of the group participate? What actions can the moderator take to facilitate participation?

8. What is a probe? List some examples and indicate how they might be used.

9. How does a moderator deal with a real expert on the topic of discussion? A self-appointed expert?

10. Why is it not usually a good idea to have friends participate in the same focus group?

11. What special problems are posed by children as focus group participants?

12. What issues must be considered when collecting observational data from focus group sessions?

13. What techniques can a moderator use to facilitate discussion of sensitive or embarrassing topics?

14. What challenges arise when conducting focus groups in an international environment? How might these challenges be overcome?

15. What is a virtual focus group? When might these groups be especially useful?

Exercise: Assemble a group of four or five acquaintances and select a topic for discussion. Moderate a 20-minute discussion of the topic.

7

Analyzing Focus Group Data

The analysis and interpretation of focus group data require a great deal of judgment and care, just as any other scientific approach, and regardless of whether the analysis relies on quantitative or qualitative procedures. A great deal of the skepticism about the value of focus groups probably arises from the perception that focus group data are subjective and difficult to interpret. However, the analysis and interpretation of focus group data can be as rigorous as that generated by any other method. It can even be quantified and submitted to sophisticated mathematical analyses, though the purposes of focus group interviews seldom require this type of analysis. Indeed, there is no one best or correct approach to the analysis of focus group data. As with other types of data, the nature of the analyses of focus group interview data should be determined by the research question and the purpose for which the data are collected.

The most common purpose of a focus group interview is to provide an in-depth exploration of a topic about which little is known. For such exploratory research, a simple descriptive narrative is quite appropriate and often all that is necessary. More detailed analyses are simply neither an efficient or productive use of time, unless they serve a particular research objective. However, there are additional methods of analysis that may be appropriate for certain purposes. In this chapter, we consider the methods of data analysis that are most frequently used with focus group data. We begin this discussion by considering the question of how much analysis is appropriate.

HOW MUCH ANALYSIS?

Like most types of research, the amount of analysis required varies with the purpose of the research, the complexity of the research design, and the extent to which conclusions can be reached easily based on simple analyses. The most common analyses of focus group results involve a transcript of the discussion and a summary of the conclusions that can be drawn. There are occasions, however, when a transcript is unnecessary. When decisions must be made quickly (which is common in marketing studies) and the conclusions of the research are rather straightforward, a brief summary may be all that is necessary. In some cases, there may be time or budget constraints that prevent more detailed analysis. In other cases, all interested parties and decision makers may be able to observe or participate in the group, so there may be little need for a detailed analysis or report. Nevertheless, some type of report is almost always helpful, if only to document what was done for historical and auditing purposes.

When the results of a focus group are so obvious as to require little supporting documentation, detailed analysis is probably not worthwhile. One of the authors was involved in a series of focus groups on a new government program that was so clearly unacceptable and elicited so many objections that further analysis of any kind seemed unwarranted. In this case, the decision about the program was made quite clear by the focus group discussions. This is, in fact, a good example of how useful focus groups can be as evaluative tools. It is often the case that government planners, product design engineers, and other professionals who design products and services believe that they understand what their clients or customers need or should want. Focus groups provide a tool for testing the reality of assumptions that go into the design of services, programs, and products. On the other hand, if the researchers in this example were interested in more than making a simple go/no go decision about a product or program and instead wished to explore in detail the reasons the program was unacceptable and the types of programs that might be acceptable, more detailed analyses would be needed. Thus, the amount of analysis and the level of detail and rigor ultimately depend on the purpose for which the research is carried out and the cost-benefit of carrying out an analysis at a given level.

Aside from the few occasions when only a short summary of focus group discussions is required, all analytic techniques for focus group data require transcription of the interview as a first step. Thus we consider the issues surrounding the transcription process and then turn our attention to some of the more common tools for analysis of focus group data.

TRANSCRIBING THE INTERVIEW

The first step in many approaches to the analysis of focus group data is to have the entire interview transcribed. Transcription services are readily available in most cities and are generally able to provide relatively rapid turnaround at modest cost. Transcription not only facilitates further analysis, but also it establishes a permanent written record of the group discussion that can be shared with other interested parties. On the other hand, in research situations that are time pressured or involve fairly mundane issues (e.g., advertising copy testing), a transcript may not be prepared. In these cases, the researchers rely on detailed notes taken by the focus group observers, or they may also replay the audio- or videotape of the group as needed.

The amount of editing that the analyst does on a transcribed interview is a matter of preference. Transcriptions are not always complete, and the moderator may want to fill in gaps and missing words, as well as correct spelling and typographical errors. There is a danger in this, of course, because the moderator's memory may be fallible or knowledge of what was said later in the course of the interview may color the memory of what happened earlier.

Transcription also will faithfully pick up incomplete sentences, half-finished thoughts, parts of words, odd phrases, and other characteristics of the spoken word in a group discussion. These characteristics are true to the flow of the discussion, but they may make it difficult for a reader to follow the text. Some editing may increase readability, but it is important that the character of the respondents' comments be maintained, even if at times they use poor grammar or appear to be confused. Because one use of focus group interviewing is to learn how respondents' think and talk about a particular issue, too much editing and cleaning of the transcript is undesirable and counterproductive.

Once the transcript is finished, it can serve as the basis for further analysis. It should be noted, however, that the transcript does not reflect the entire character of the discussion. Nonverbal communication, gestures, and behavioral responses are not reflected in a transcript. In addition, the way members of the group use words and the tone with which words are used are important sources of information and can radically alter the interpretation of a statement. The statement, "That is bad," can have several very different meanings. The word *bad* is sometimes used as a way to say something is actually very good. Such a statement could also mean something is really bad in the traditional meaning of this word.

For these reasons, the interviewer or observer may wish to supplement the transcript with some additional observational data that were obtained during the interview. Such data may include notes that the interviewer or observers made during the interview, the systematic recording of specific events and behaviors by trained observers, or the content analysis of videotapes of the discussion. Such observational data may be quite useful, but it will only be available if its collection was planned in advance. Preplanning of the analyses of the data to be obtained from focus groups is as important as it is for any other type of research. Once the focus group discussions have been transcribed, analysis can begin. Today researchers have a variety of choices in analyzing focus group data, and these generally fall into two basic categories: qualitative or quantitative. Because focus groups are a variety of qualitative research, the following discussion examines qualitative analytic approaches.

QUALITATIVE ANALYTIC APPROACHES

Technological advances in statistics have enabled extensive and elaborate analyses of huge data bases derived from surveys, retail transactions, census data, and numerous other sources. As later sections in this chapter explain, quantitative analyses can also be applied effectively to qualitative data obtained from individual depth interviews, focus groups, and ethnographies. On the other hand, studies that rely on qualitative research methods often employ qualitative approaches to extracting meaning from the data. Unfortunately, unlike most statistical paradigms, there is much less consensus on how to analyze and interpret qualitative data. To a considerable degree, this is the result of differences in the epistemological orientations and phenomenological foci that characterize the behavioral science disciplines.

Epistemological Orientation

Whether explicit or simply subsumed, disciplines adopt basic premises about the sources and nature of knowledge. Three distinctive perspectives are particularly relevant to qualitative analyses of focus group data (Sayre, 2001). First, social constructivism broadly posits that much of reality and the meaning and categories that frame everyday life are essentially social creations. This orientation traces its origins to thinking from social psychology, sociology, and cultural anthropology. Focus group analyses that reflect this view tend to emphasize how group members collaborate on some issue, how they achieve consensus (or fail to), and how they construct shared meanings about commercial products, communications, or social concerns. The phenomenological approach to analysis is almost the opposite. Drawing generally from clinical psychology and more specifically from phenomenological psychology, the analytic emphasis is on the subjective, idiosyncratic perceptions and motivations of the individual respondent. This perspective is particularly useful in marketing focus groups in which managers are extremely interested, for example, in the detailed and in-depth reasons why one person loves the new flavor of Fritos and another group member finds it disgusting. Because both individuals represent important segments, thoroughly mining their thoughts and feelings is critical. Finally, advocates of interpretivism accept the prior perspectives but are skeptical about taking focus group respondents' words at face value. Researchers from this school owe much to ethnographic studies that focus on both individuals' words and actions, particularly to the science of body language and facial expressions.

Disciplinary Focus

As discussed in Chapter 1, the ways in which the earliest focus groups were designed, fielded, and analyzed were strongly influenced by their parent disciplines, particularly social and clinical psychology and marketing research. These influences remain strong today, although much cross-disciplinary evolution has blurred some of the original differences. Newer intellectual currents have also affected how researchers analyze focus group data. The field of hermeneutics migrated from Europe to the American consumer research community in the 1980s. It values consumer stories, or narratives, as a powerful tool for understanding consumer motivation, meaning, and decision making. Consumers' verbal expressions are conceptualized as "text" and interpreted through an iterative process of reading, analyzing, and rereading the text. For a review of the hermeneutic approach, see Thompson (1997). The field of semiotics also focuses on textual data but interprets this more broadly as including not only verbal expressions but pictures, sounds, products, and advertisements (Sayre, 2001, p. 210). Semiotic analyses commonly deconstruct textual data to uncover unintended or hidden messages, which has proved particularly useful in the field of advertising and communications research (McQuarrie & Mick, 1996; Stern, 1995). More broadly, semiotic analyses of qualitative consumer data have helped identify the signs and symbols that are embedded in textual data (Umiker-Sebeok, 1987). Finally, some approaches to analyzing focus group data are, in comparison with hermeneutics and semiotics, relatively atheoretical. This is particularly true of marketing studies that seek to discover the major ideas and themes that emerge from the group discussion. This approach also serves marketers' frequent need to quantify, statistically analyze, and generalize the findings from small-sample qualitative studies.

Workbench Issues

Regardless of the disciplinary orientation of the focus group researcher, there are common everyday issues that arise during many groups and require analytic attention. Unlike statistical studies, focus group analysis actually begins once the group has begun. This is due largely to the discretionary opportunities the moderator has to terminate a topic, expand the discussion on one that the group finds involving, or introduce an entirely new line of questioning. Still, the main analytic work occurs after the focus group discussion ends. Above and beyond the hard data provided by the transcript, qualitative analyses of focus groups involve other often equally important considerations.

The following draws from discussion in A. E. Goldman and McDonald (1987, pp. 164–166).

Issue Order

Focus group discussions commonly begin with open-ended "grand tour" questions that seek to obtain participants' overall orientation toward a topic. The moderator might begin with questions like, "Tell me about your overall grocery shopping experiences these days," or "How do you feel about your health insurance plan?" It is often analytically interesting to observe which aspects are top-of-mind and expressed first in the discussion. Judgment is required to interpret whether the issues that are raised first truly represent the participants' major concerns or are merely mundane and socially safe topics. For example, in responding to the question about grocery shopping, someone might complain about the high prices when this is actually not a major issue, but it represents a conventional perspective and an easy way of joining the discussion.

Issue Absence or Presence

Most analyses of focus group data seek to find meaning in the nature of participants' verbal or written responses to the questions in the discussion guide. This is logical and necessary, but exclusive emphasis on what is said or written may provide only a partial picture of the situation. Things that go unsaid or are not raised in the discussion may be equally important. Some issues that participants don't address may simply represent things that are taken for granted (e.g., clean restrooms in restaurants). Others may represent socially sensitive topics that individuals would prefer to avoid (e.g., retirement savings activities and strategies). Finally, other issues may not materialize in the discussion because they are simply not important. Interpreting the significance of things that go unsaid requires considerable skills on the part of both the moderator and the analyst(s).

Time Spent on the Issue

In preparing a focus group discussion guide, researchers typically allocate blocks of time to the topics that will be covered. It is not surprising that things don't always go as planned. Some questions that were anticipated to elicit extensive discussion fall flat and yield pithy sound bites from indifferent respondents. Conversely, minor or transitional questions sometimes stimulate vigorous wide-ranging discussion and much interaction among the participants.

This tends to frustrate the moderator, but more important, it provides clues to how much the participants care about a particular issue. It may be misleading to focus only on the responses to different questions without also considering the amount of time the participants chose to spend on each one.

Intensity of Expression

Often related to the issue of time are the moods and emotions that arise as various topics are covered. A focus group can be like an emotional roller coaster that veers from the dull formality of a committee meeting to moments of group hilarity to mildly hostile silence. Such situations challenge the moderator to get things going or calm them down. They also challenge the analyst to interpret the nature and sources of participants' emotional reactions and expressions. The field of marketing today places a strong emphasis on the theory and practice of customer relationship management (CRM). The role of consumers' emotional connections to products and brands is increasingly seen as a key link in the relationship. This orientation has contributed to the growing use in focus groups of emotional elicitation techniques such as projective methods.

Reasons Versus Reactions

Focus group analysts are naturally interested in observing how participants react to the various questions and stimuli that are presented to the group. Sometimes when discussion guides are crammed with too many questions, the moderator is pressed just to get through them all and has little time for probing the participants about the reasons for their responses. In other situations, which are quite common in marketing studies, the researchers have a strong interest in separating winning from losing product or advertising concepts. Such groups tend to involve a lot of voting and ranking from the participants, and they often pay insufficient attention to the various and often subtle reasons for their evaluations. Overemphasis on individuals' reactions is at odds with the basic premise of focus group research that, ideally, mines rather than surveys participants' ideas and orientations.

Doubt and Disbelief

One central theme in the current criticism of focus group research is that participants say one thing and do another. This problem is not unique to focus groups and also arises in survey research. Focus group moderators and analysts need to be sensitive to situations in which participants' expressions may reflect social desirability influences, pressures to conform to groupthink, or the persuasive effects of a dominant group member. The analysis also needs to be aware of and seek to resolve individual responses that are inconsistent. For example, in a focus group comprised of mothers of young children, one person explained, "I check the nutrition labels very carefully on the food I buy for my kids," yet later in the group, the same woman said, "Sometimes, if the kids like it, I just throw it in the cart. I always seem to be in a hurry." Focus group researchers often need to exercise caution in accepting participants' words at face value.

Individuals Versus the Group

The analysis of focus group data often seeks to generalize findings in terms of the group using terms such as *most, very few,* and *the majority.* In groups that are extremely homogeneous (e.g., upper-middle-class widows between 65 and 75 years old who still live independently), this may make sense. On the other hand, it represents a subtle intrusion of inappropriate quantitative analysis. In most studies, focus group research involves small samples that are imperfectly representative of a larger population. This makes group level generalizations questionable on both statistical and sampling criteria. An alternative approach is to view each individual in the group as representing a particular demographic, lifestyle, or attitudinal segment, which encourages a within-person rather than an across-person analysis.

The Scissor-and-Sort Technique

The scissor-and-sort technique, which is sometimes called the cut-and-paste method, is a quick and cost-effective method for analyzing a transcript of a focus group discussion. The first step in applying the technique is to go through the transcript and identify those sections of it that are relevant to the research question(s). Based on this initial reading, a classification system for major topics and issues is developed, and material in the transcript related to each topic is identified. Color-coded brackets or symbols may be used to mark different topics within the text with colors. The amount of material coded for any one topic depends on the importance of that topic to the overall research question and the amount of variation in the discussion. The coded material may be phrases, sentences, or long exchanges between individual respondents. The only requirement is that the material be relevant to the particular category with which it has been identified. This coding exercise may require several passes through the transcript as categories of topics evolve and the analyst gains greater insight into the content of the group discussion.

Once the coding process is complete, the coded copy of the transcribed interview may be cut apart (the scissors part of the technique). Each piece of coded material can be cut out and sorted so that all material relevant to a particular topic is placed together. This cutting and sorting process may also be readily carried out on any computer with a word-processing program. Whether scissors or a personal computer is employed in the process, both yield a set of sorted materials that provides the basis for developing a summary report. Each topic is treated in turn with a brief introduction. The various pieces of transcribed text are used as supporting materials and incorporated within an interpretative analysis.

The scissor-and-sort technique is a very useful and efficient approach to analysis, but it does tend to rely very heavily on the judgment of a single analyst. This analyst determines which segments of the transcript are important, develops a categorization system for the topics discussed by the group, selects representative statements regarding these topics from the transcript, and develops an interpretation of what it all means. There is obviously much opportunity for subjectivity and potential bias in this approach. Yet, it shares many of the characteristics of more sophisticated and time-consuming approaches.

In some cases, it may be desirable to have two or more analysts independently code the focus group transcript. The use of multiple analysts provides an opportunity to assess the reliability of coding, at least with respect to major themes and issues. When determining the reliability of more detailed types of codes such as the intensity of positive and negative emotion associated with various institutions and organizations, more sophisticated coding procedures are required. All are types of content analysis, a topic to which we now turn.

Content Analysis

The meaning of a focus group discussion, or for that matter any set of words, does not leap out complete with interpretation and insight. Rather, the content of the discussion must be examined and the meaning and its particular implications for the research question at hand discovered. Every effort to interpret a focus group represents analysis of content. There are, however, rigorous approaches to the analysis of content, approaches that emphasize the reliability and replicability of observations and subsequent interpretation. These approaches include a variety of specific methods and techniques that are collectively known as content analysis (Krippendorf, 2004). There are frequent occasions when the use of this more rigorous approach is appropriate for the analysis of data generated by focus groups. This may even be necessary when numerous focus groups are fielded, yielding a large volume of data.

The literature on content analysis provides the foundation for computer-assisted approaches to the analysis of focus group data. Computer-assisted approaches to content analysis are increasingly being applied to focus group data because they maintain much of the rigor of traditional content analysis while greatly reducing the time and cost required to complete such analyses. Such programs also provide a means for examining the contents of verbal interaction in ways that are impossible for a human observer. We consider computer-assisted approaches to content analysis in detail later in this chapter. Before doing so, however, it will be helpful to more rigorously define content analysis and review the general approach employed in such analysis.

Krippendorf (2004) defined content analysis as "a research technique for making replicable and valid inferences from texts (or other meaningful matter) to the contexts of their use" (p. 18). Over 40 years ago, Janis (1965) defined it as follows:

> Any technique (a) for the classification of the sign-vehicles (b) which relies solely upon the judgments (which theoretically may range from perceptual discrimination to sheer guesses) of an analyst or group of analysts as to which sign-vehicles fall into which categories, (c) provided that the analyst's judgments are regarded as the report of a scientific observer. (p. 55)

A *sign-vehicle* is anything that may carry meaning, though most often it is likely to be a word or set of words in the context of a focus group interview. Sign-vehicles may also include gestures, facial expressions, tone of voice, or any of a variety of other means of communication, however. Indeed, such nonverbal signs may carry a great deal of information and should not be overlooked as a source of information.

Content analysis has a long and rich history in the social sciences (see Krippendorf, 2004, for a concise history of the method). It has been widely applied to such varied phenomena as propaganda, literature and newspapers, transcripts of psychotherapy sessions, and television programming. A rather substantial body of literature now exists on content analysis including books by Krippendorf (2004), Neuendorf (2002; see http://academic.csuohio.edu/ kneuendorf/content/ for an online version of this source), and Popping (2002). A number of specific instruments have been developed to facilitate content analysis including the Message Measurement Inventory (R. G. Smith, 1978) and the Gottschalk-Gleser Content Analysis Scale (Gottschalk, Winget, & Gleser, 1969). The Message Measurement Inventory was originally designed for the analysis of communications in the mass media, such as television programming and news magazines. The Gottschalk-Gleser Content Analysis Scale, on the other hand, was designed for the analysis of interpersonal communication. Both scales have been in use for a long time, and there is a rich literature on their applications. These scales have been adapted for other purposes, but they are generally representative of the types of formal content analysis scales that are in use.

Janis (1965) identified three distinct types of content analysis based on the purpose of the investigation:

1. *Pragmatical content analysis,* which includes procedures for classifying signs according to their probable causes and effects. In this type of analysis the emphasis is on why something is said.

2. *Semantical content analysis,* which seeks to classify signs according to their meanings. This type of analysis may take three forms:

   a. *Designation analysis,* which determines the frequency with which certain objects (or persons, institutions, or concepts) are mentioned. This type of analysis can be a rather simple counting exercise.

   b. *Attribution analysis,* which examines the frequency with which certain characterizations or descriptors are used. Again, this can be a simple counting exercise, but the emphasis is on adjectives, adverbs, descriptive phrases, and qualifiers rather than the targets of these parts of speech.

   c. *Assertions analysis,* which provides the frequency with which certain objects (persons, institutions, etc.) are characterized in a particular way. Assertions analysis involves combining designation analysis and attribution analysis. Such an analysis often takes the form of a matrix, with objects as columns and descriptors as rows.

3. *Sign-vehicle analysis,* which classifies content according to the psychophysical properties of signs (counting the number of times specific words or types of words are used). For example, the degree to which a topic is emotionally involving for respondents may be revealed by examination of the number of emotion-laden words used. (p. 57)

All of these types of analysis may be appropriate to the analysis of focus group data depending on the types of research questions at issue. For example, pragmatical content analysis may be employed when trying to understand the attributions of a group of consumers concerning product failures or the beliefs of a group of teenagers concerning the transmission of AIDS. Semantical content analysis might be used to look at the number of positive and negative characterizations of the Democratic or Republican Party. This example is more specifically an assertions analysis. Finally, sign-vehicle analysis might be used to count the number of emotion-laden words that a group of union members use when referring to their employers. Indeed, these are examples of three measures that have a long history of use: (a) the frequency with which a symbol or idea appears, which tends to be interpreted as a measure of importance, attention, or emphasis; (b) the relative balance of favorable and unfavorable attributions regarding a symbol or idea, which tends to be interpreted as a measure of direction or bias; and (c) the kinds of qualifications and associations made with respect to a symbol or idea, which tend to be interpreted as a measure of the intensity of belief or conviction (Krippendorf, 2004, p. 59). Other types of measures that may flow from these types of analyses might focus on the presence or absence of an idea or concept, which might suggest something about focus group respondents' awareness or knowledge and the frequency with which two or more ideas, objects, or persons are associated or linked (Krippendorf, 2004, p. 59).

Although content analysis is a specific type of research tool, it shares many features with other types of research. The same stages of the research process found in content analysis are present in any research project. Krippendorf (2004, p. 83f) identified a number of these stages:

- Data making
- Data reduction
- Inference
- Analysis
- Validation
- Testing for correspondence with other methods
- Testing hypotheses regarding other data

Data used in content analysis include human speech, observations of behavior, and various forms of nonverbal communication. The speech itself may be recorded, and if video cameras are used, at least some of the behavior and nonverbal communication may be permanently archived. Such data are highly unstructured, however, at least for the purposes of the researcher. Before the content of a focus group can be analyzed, it must be converted into specific units of information that can be analyzed by the researcher. The particular organizing structure that may be used will depend on the particular purpose of the research, but there are specific steps in the structuring process that are common to all applications and questions. These steps are unitizing, sampling, and recording.

Unitizing involves defining the appropriate unit or level of analysis. It would be possible to consider each word spoken in a focus group as a unit for analysis. Alternatively, the unit of analysis could be a sentence, a sequence of sentences, or a complete dialogue about a particular topic. Krippendorf (2004, pp. 97–110) suggested that in content analysis there are three kinds of units that must be considered: sampling units, recording units, and context units.

Sampling units are those parts of the larger whole that can be regarded as independent of each other. Sampling units tend to have physically identified boundaries. For example, sampling units may be defined as individual words, complete statements of an individual, or the totality of an exchange among two or more individuals.

Recording units, on the other hand, tend to grow out of the descriptive system that is being employed. Generally, recording units are subsets of sampling units. For example, the set of words with emotional connotations would describe certain types of words and would be a subset of the total words used. Alternatively, individual statements of several group members may be recording units that make up a sampling unit that consists of all of the verbal exchanges related to a particular topic or issue. In this latter case, the recording units might provide a means for describing those exchanges that are, for example, hostile, supportive, or friendly.

Context units provide a basis for interpreting a recording unit. They may be identical to recording units in some cases, whereas in other cases they may be quite independent. Context units are often defined in terms of the syntax or structure in which a recording unit occurs. For example, in marketing research, it is often useful to learn how frequently evaluative words are used in the context of describing a particular product or service. Thus, context units provide a referent for the content of the recording units. To illustrate how these distinctions might be drawn in a particular study, consider a medical equipment manufacturer that is exploring new product opportunities through several focus groups. The context unit is a new in-home medical device that enables the early diagnosis of diabetes. The sampling units would be participants' words or phrases and the recording units their expressions of positive or negative attitudes about the medical product.

Sampling units, then, represent the way in which the broad structure of the information within the discussion is divided. Sampling units provide a way of organizing information that is related. Within these broader sampling units, the recording units represent specific statements, and the context units represent the environment or context in which the statement occurs. The way in which these units are defined can have a significant influence on the interpretation of the content of a particular focus group discussion. These units can be defined in a number of different ways. Table 7.1 distinguishes five such approaches to defining these units. Focus group research is most often concerned with referential, propositional, and thematic units, but there may be occasions when the use of physical or syntactical units is appropriate. This approach may seem somewhat abstract and overlapping to some degree, yet it provides a framework for more systematic and nuanced analyses of focus group data. Also, the definition of the appropriate unit of analysis must be driven by both the purpose of the research and the ability of the researcher to achieve reliability in the coding system. The reliability of such coding systems must be determined empirically and in many cases involves the use of measures of interrater agreement.

TABLE 7.1
Approaches to Defining Content Units

- *Physical units* divide the content of a medium by such physical properties as size, place, time, and length. For example, a book, a billboard, and a single issue of a magazine would all be examples of physical units. The boundaries of these units are defined by time and space.

- *Syntactical units* divide the content of a medium based on its natural grammar. Words, individual television programs or news items, and chapters within books are examples. These units tend to be defined by the source of the communication.

- *Categorical units* are defined in terms of a referent, an expression, regardless of length, that refers to or describes the same person, object, or event.

- *Propositional units* (also called kernels) are referential units that possess a particular structure and offer a particular thought about the referent object or person. Thus, the statement, "He is a bright, but dishonest man," includes two propositions: (a) the man is bright and (b) the man is dishonest.

- *Thematic units* include more global interpretative or explanatory sets of statements. Recurring systems of beliefs or explanations represent thematic units. Thus, one might find that in a focus group there is a recurring theme that salespeople are dishonest. Alternatively, analysis of the morning news over time might reveal themes related to significant economic changes or political conflict.

SOURCE: Adapted from Krippendorf (2004), pp. 97–110.

It is seldom practical or necessary to try to unitize all of the discussion that arises in a focus group. When multiple focus groups are carried out on the same general topic, complete unitization becomes even more difficult. For this reason, most content analyses of focus groups involve some sampling of the total group discussion for purposes of analysis. The analyst may seek to identify important themes and sample statements within a theme or use some other approach such as examining statements made in response to particular types of questions or at particular points in the conversation. Like other types of sampling, the intent of sampling in content analysis is to provide a representative subset of the larger population. It is relatively easy to draw incorrect conclusions from a focus group if care is not taken to ensure representative sampling of the content of the group discussion. Almost any contention can be supported by taking a set of numerically unrepresentative statements out of the context in which they were spoken. Thus, it is important for the analyst to devise a plan for sampling the total content of group discussions. This task is complicated when only some group participants answer a particular question.

The final stage of data making is the recording of the data in such a way as to ensure their reliability and meaningfulness. The recording phase of content analysis is not simply the rewriting of the statements of one or more respondents. Rather, it is the use of the defined units of analysis to classify the content of the discussion into categories such that the meaning of the discussions is maintained and explicated. It is only after this latter stage has been accomplished that one can claim to actually have data for purposes of analysis and interpretation.

The recording phase of content analysis requires the execution of an explicit set of recording instructions. These instructions represent the rules for assigning units (words, phrases, sentences, gestures, etc.) to categories. These instructions must address at least four different aspects of the recording process (Krippendorf, 2004):

1. The nature of the raw data from which the recording is to be done (transcript, tape recording, film, etc.)
2. The characteristics of coders (recorders), including any special skills such as familiarity with the subject matter and scientific research
3. The training that coders will need in order to do the recording
4. The specific rules for placing units into categories

These rules are critical to establishing the reliability of the recording exercise and the entire data-making process. Further, it is necessary that these rules be made explicit and that they are demonstrated to produce reliable results when used by individuals other than those who developed them in the first place. The common practice of reporting high interrater reliability coefficients when they are based solely on the agreement of individuals who have worked closely together to develop a coding system does not provide a fair and reasonable measure of reliability (Lorr & McNair, 1966). Rather, the minimum requirement for establishing the reliability of a coding system should be a demonstration that judges exhibit substantial agreement when using only the coding rules.

Once a set of recording rules has been defined and demonstrated to produce reliable results, the data-making process can be completed by applying the recording rules to the full content of the material of interest. Under ideal circumstances, recording will involve more than one judge so that the coding of each specific unit can be examined for reliability and sources of disagreement can be identified and corrected. This is because there is a difference between developing a generally reliable set of recording rules and ensuring that an individual element in a transcript is reliably coded.

The assessment of the reliability of a coding system may be carried out in a variety of ways. As noted above, there is a difference between establishing that multiple recorders are in general agreement (manifest a high degree of inter-rater reliability) and establishing that a particular unit is reliably coded. The researcher must decide which approach is more useful for the given research question. In most focus group projects, general rater reliability will be more important because the emphasis is on general themes in the group discussion rather than specific units. However, there may be occasions when the reliability of individual units is more relevant.

Computation of a coefficient of agreement provides a quantitative index of the reliability of the recording system. There exists a substantial literature on coefficients of agreement. Treatment of this literature and issues related to the selection of a specific coefficient of agreement are beyond the scope of this book. Among the more common coefficients in use are kappa (Cohen, 1956), pi (Scott, 1955), and Krippendorf's alpha (Krippendorf, 1970, 2004). All of these coefficients correct the observed level of agreement (or disagreement) for the level that would be expected by chance alone. Krippendorf (2004) offers a useful discussion of reliability coefficients in content analysis, including procedures for use with more than two judges (see also Spiegelman, Terwilliger, & Fearing, 1953).

Data making tends to be the most time-consuming of all the stages in content analysis. It is also the stage that has received the greatest attention in the content analysis literature. The reason for this is that content analysis involves data making after observations have been obtained rather than before. Content analysis uses the observations themselves to suggest what should be examined and submitted to further analysis, whereas many other types of research establish the specific domain(s) of interest and associated metrics prior to observation.

The difference in the emphasis accorded the data-making phase by different types of research methods is similar to the difference between essay questions and multiple-choice questions. In both types of questions, there are certain issues of interest, but in the case of essay questions, the answers are not provided. Thus, the answers are in the words of the respondent. Whoever evaluates the examination must devote time to analyzing the answers and determining how "correct" the response is. This evaluation stage is unnecessary for multiple-choice questions because the available answers are identified for the respondent, and the evaluator need only determine whether the correct answer was selected. Multiple-choice questions require greater preparation prior to administration because the correct answer must be identified along with reasonable alternative, but incorrect, responses.

In survey research, much of the data making occurs prior to administration of the survey. Such data making involves identification of reasonable alternatives from which a respondent selects an answer. Thus, data making is a step in survey research and all types of research, but it occurs prior to observation. In content analysis, data making occurs after observation. The emphasis on reliability is clearly important in studies with scientific, theoretical purposes. On the other hand, these procedures are used less frequently in the time-pressured and pragmatic focus groups that are conducted in the marketing research field.

QUANTITATIVE ANALYSIS

The recording or coding of individual units is not content analysis. It is merely a first stage in preparation for analysis. The specific types of analyses that might be used in a given application will depend on the purpose of the research. Virtually any analytic tool may be employed, ranging from simple descriptive analysis to more elaborate data reduction and multivariate associative techniques. Much of the content analysis work that occurs in the context of focus group data tends to be descriptive, but this need not be the case. Indeed, although focus group data tend to be regarded as qualitative, proper content analysis of the data can make them amenable to the most sophisticated quantitative analysis.

It is common for focus group interviews to be used for purposes of developing hypotheses that are then tested or validated with other types of research. For example, a focus group may yield hypotheses that are tested through a survey of the population of interest. This is, of course, a perfectly appropriate approach. On the other hand, the need for validation is not unique to focus group research. This is well illustrated in a study by Reid, Soley, and Wimmer (1980) of replication studies in the field of advertising. Although the majority of the studies they examined in this research were replications of survey and experimental research findings, there was an equal probability of the replication producing results contrary to the original study as there was of the replication finding support for the original study. Such findings are not unique to advertising and suggest that replication and validation are necessary steps in any scientific endeavor. There is a need for validation of focus group results, just as there is a need for validation of other types of research findings. Such validation may involve content analysis of additional focus group data or may employ other methods and measures such as survey research or formal experiments.

COMPUTER-ASSISTED CONTENT ANALYSIS

Content analysts were quick to recognize the value of the computer as an analytical tool. The time-consuming and tedious task of data making can be greatly facilitated through use of the computer. Computers can be programmed to follow the data-making rules described earlier. The importance of ensuring that these rules are well designed is made even clearer in the context of their use by a computer. In recent years, computer-assisted interpretation of focus group interviews has received considerable attention and built on the earlier foundations of research on content analysis.

The earliest uses of computers in content analysis involved counting and sorting units of analysis. A straightforward counting of the number of words and number of different words is easily programmed on a computer, and the program can be written to ignore grammatical endings and count only different word stems. Such counts and listings are useful in data making because they provide an indication of the word content of material. Once particular categories of words have been defined, the computer can quickly count words in these identified categories and be used to quickly identify their location. Search-and-find and cut-and-paste routines that now exist on virtually every word-processing software package make it easy to automate the old cut-and-paste technique described above, which commonly saves both research time and money.

Commercial software products specifically designed for content coding and word counting are now widely available. SPSS offers a product called Verbastat (www.spss.com/verbastat/), StatPac offers a product called Verbatim Blaster (www.statpac.com/content-analysis.htm), and QSR International offers the NVivo and NUD*IST products (www.qsrinternational.com/). There are many other products available, and all vary in terms of their ease of use, comprehensiveness, focus, and cost. An especially useful review of these products is provided by Duriau and Reger (2004).

The computer is capable of a great deal more than automation of search, find, count, cut, and paste activities. One problem with simple counting and sorting of words is that these procedures lose the context in which the words occur. For example, a simple count of the frequency with which emotionally charged words are used loses information about the objects of those emotional words. Because the meanings of words are frequently context dependent, it is useful to try to capture their context. This is one reason content analysts recommend the identification and coding of context units as a routine part of content analysis.

One computer-assisted approach to capturing the context as well as content of a passage of text is the key-word-in-context (KWIC) technique. The KWIC approach searches for key words and lists the key word along with the text that surrounds it. The amount of text obtained on either side of the key word can be controlled by specification of the number of words or letters to be printed. One of the earliest computer programs for KWIC analyses was the General Inquirer (Stone, Dunphy, Smith, & Ogilvie, 1966; Stone & Hunt, 1963), which is still in use today. The home page can be found at www.wjh.harvard.edu/~inquirer/.

The General Inquirer uses a theoretically derived dictionary for classifying words. A variety of similar systems has since been developed and often uses specially designed dictionaries for a particular application. Some of these programs are simply designated as KWIC and others are named for particular applications for which KWIC may be used. Among the more frequently cited software programs for content analysis are TEXTPACK (Mohler & Zuell, 1998), about which we will have more to say shortly, Concordance (Watt, 2004), WORDSTAT (Provalis Research, 2005), and TextQuest (Social Science Consulting, 2005). Software for text analysis is frequently reviewed in journals such as *Computers and the Humanities,* published by Kluwer Academic Publishers, and *Literary and Linguistic Computing,* published by Oxford University Press. Specialized dictionaries for use in conjunction with text analysis programs like the General Inquirer and TEXTPACK are also available. Antworth and Valentine (1998) provide a brief introduction to several of these specialized programs and dictionaries.

More recent work on content analysis, built on the research on artificial intelligence and in cognitive science, recognizes that associations among words are often important determinants of meaning. Further, meaning may be related to the frequency of association of certain words, the distance between associated words or concepts (often measured by the number of intervening words), and the number of different associations. The basic idea in this work is that the way people use language provides insights into the way people organize information, impressions, and feelings in memory and, thus, how they tend to think.

The view that language provides insight into the way individuals think about the world has existed for many years. The anthropologist Edward Sapir (1929) noted that language plays a critical role in how people experience the world. Social psychologists have also long had an interest in the role language plays in the assignment of meaning and in adjustment to the environment (see for example, Bruner, Goodnow, & Austin, 1956; Chomsky, 1965; Sherif & Sherif, 1969). In more recent years, the study of categorization has become a discipline in its own right and has benefited from research on naturalistic categories in anthropology, philosophy, and developmental psychology and the work on modeling natural concepts that has occurred in the areas of semantic memory and artificial intelligence (for reviews of this literature, see Hahn & Ramscar, 2001; Medin, Lynch, & Solomon, 2000).

This research has been extended to the examination of focus groups. Building on theoretical work in the cognitive sciences, Anderson (1983), Grunert (1982), and Grunert and Goder (1986) developed a computer-assisted procedure

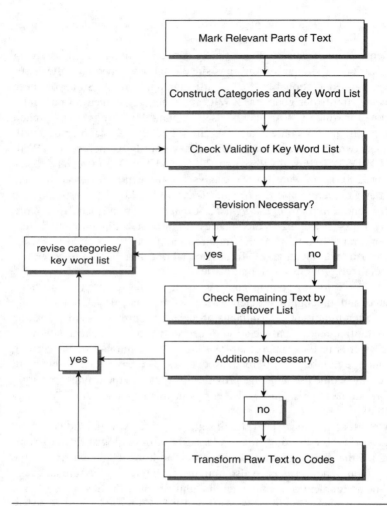

Figure 7.1   Data Making Prior to Analysis of Associative Proximities

SOURCE: Grunert and Goder (1986). Reprinted with permission.

for analyzing the proximities of word associations. Their approach builds on prior work on content analysis as well. Indeed, the data-making phase of the approach, which is illustrated in Figure 7.1, uses the KWIC approach as an interactive tool for designing a customized dictionary of categories. The particular computer program used for this purpose is TEXTPACK, but other computer packages are also available.

The construction of a customized dictionary of categories is particularly important for the content analysis of focus groups because the range and specificity of topics that may be dealt with by focus group interviews is very broad, and no general purpose dictionary or set of codes and categories is likely to suit the purposes of a researcher with a specific research application. For example, in focus groups designed to examine the ways in which groups of respondents think and talk about personal computers, there will be a need to develop a dictionary of categories that refer specifically to the features of computers, particular applications, and specific work environments. In focus groups designed to examine the use of condoms among inner city adolescents, it is likely that a dictionary of categories will be required to capture the content of the discussion that includes the slang vernacular of the respondents. Although the dictionaries developed for other applications may provide some helpful suggestions, the specificity of the language used by particular groups of respondents to discuss a specific object within a given context almost always means that the focus group analyst will have to develop a customized categorization system. Although quantitative in approach, such procedures enhance focus groups' qualitative objective to obtain the natural language and expressions of individual participants.

Once the data-making phase is complete, the associative structure of the discussion content can be analyzed. This is accomplished by counting the distances between various cognitive categories. Distance, or the proximity of two categories of content, is defined as the number of intervening constructs. Thus two constructs that appear next to one another would have a distance of 1. To simplify computations, Grunert and Goder (1986) recommended examining categories that are at a maximum value of 10. This maximum value is then used as a reference point and distances are subtracted from it in order to obtain a numeric value that varies directly (rather than inversely) with intensity of association. This procedure yields a proximity value rather than a distance measure; that is, the higher scores represent closer associations among categories. Because most categories appear more than once, the measures of association are summed over all occurrences to obtain a total proximity score for each pair of constructs. These proximity data may then be used for further analysis.

Grunert and Goder (1986) provided an illustration of their procedure in the context of focus groups designed to learn something about differences in the way laypersons and experts talk and think about cameras. Focus group data obtained independently from laypersons and experts were submitted to analysis. Of particular interest were differences in the two groups with respect to associations between particular attributes of cameras and uses of cameras. More specifically, interest focused on the frequency with which particular characteristics of cameras, such as autofocus and lens variety, are mentioned

AUMA Characteristics	Laypersons	Experts
Total # of attributes	36	40
# of attributes linked to uses	13	31
Total # of uses	4	12
# of uses linked to attributes	4	12
Absolute # of links	19	120
Relative # of links	13%	25%

BAMA Characteristics	Laypersons	Experts
Total # of attributes	36	40
# of attributes linked to brands	28	34
Total # of brands	22	27
# of brands linked to attributes	20	24
Absolute # of links	151	274
Relative # of links	19%	25%

BUMA Characteristics	Laypersons	Experts
Total # of attributes	22	27
# of attributes linked to brands	0	14
Total # of brands	4	12
# of brands linked to attributes	0	10
Absolute # of links	0	34
Relative # of links	—	10%

Figure 7.2   Summary Information on Camera Associations

SOURCE: Grunert and Goder (1986). Reprinted with permission.

in the context of specific uses of cameras (represented by an attribute uses matrix [AUMA]). Also of interest were differences related to the frequency with which specific brands of cameras are mentioned in the context of uses like action photography, slides, and portraits (represented by a brand uses matrix [BUMA]). In addition, the study focused on differences between particular brands with respect to specific attributes, that is the frequency with which specific brands of cameras are associated with particular features (represented by a brand attribute matrix [BAMA]).

Figure 7.2 provides a summary of the results of this application. Not surprisingly, there are far richer associative structures among experts than among laypersons. The particular character of these structures can also be illustrated. For example, Figure 7.3 provides an illustration of the associative structures of experts and laypersons for the brand Canon. The lengths of the lines in the figure are inversely related to strength of association. The graphical illustration in Figure 7.3 provides a comprehensible means for summarizing the information obtained through content analysis. Note that Figure 7.3 provides information about the types of associations made as well as the frequency of these associations, which are represented by the numbers within the circles.

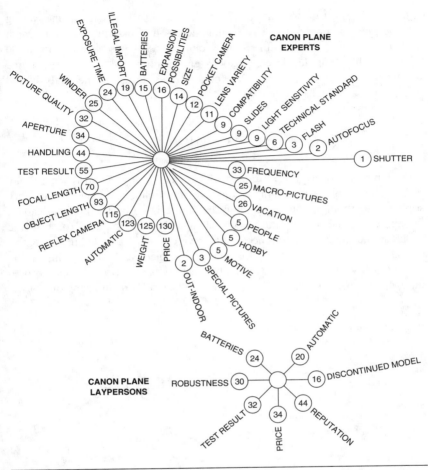

Figure 7.3 Graphic Representation of the Canon Plane for Experts and Laypersons

SOURCE: Grunert and Goder (1986). Reprinted with permission.

Obviously, the amount of effort required to complete the type of analysis summarized in Figures 7.2 and 7.3 is considerable. Whether the amount of effort is justified in other applications depends on a variety of factors: time and budget constraints, the nature of the research question, and the availability of a computer and the necessary software. The important point to be made is that the level and detail of analysis of focus group data can be increased considerably through use of the computer. At the same time, the computer can be an extremely useful tool for data reduction. It can also be used for uncovering relationships that might otherwise go unnoticed. Thus, like most of the research tools in the social sciences, the focus group interview has benefited from the advent of the computer. Users of focus group interviews have also become increasingly facile in the use of the computer as an aid to the analysis and interpretation of focus group data.

CONCLUSION

The analysis of focus group data can take a wide variety of forms. These may range from very rapid, highly subjective impressionistic analyses to very sophisticated computer-assisted analyses. There is no best approach. Rather, the approach selected should be consistent with the original purpose of the research and the information needs that gave rise to it. It is unfair to suggest that all focus group research involves highly subjective analysis. This is certainly the case in many applications, but there exist an array of sound procedures for ensuring reliable and objective results and for quantifying outcomes.

REVIEW QUESTIONS

1. What factors should be considered when determining how much analysis of a focus group discussion is worthwhile?

2. How much editing of a transcription of a focus group is useful? Why?

3. What factors should a focus group researcher consider in choosing a qualitative versus a quantitative approach?

4. Why is the order in which focus group participants raise particular topics important?

5. In what type of situation should focus group analysts be skeptical about what focus group participants say in the group?

6. Describe the scissor-and-sort technique. How can this technique be automated on the computer?

7. What is content analysis? Why is it appropriate for analysis of focus group discussions?

8. What is data making? Why is it important?

9. What are the steps in data making?

10. What are recording rules? How does one determine whether a set of rules is useful?

11. What is the key-word-in-context (KWIC) approach? How would it be used to analyze focus group data?

12. What is meant by *associative structure?* How does one examine associative structure? How might analysis of associative structures be useful in the context of focus group research?

13. Identify research situations when the following types of analysis might be most appropriate:
    a. A quick impressionistic summary
    b. A thematic analysis using the cut-and-paste approach
    c. Assertions analysis
    d. Pragmatical analysis
    e. Analysis of associative structures

Exercise: Find a news story in a popular magazine. Develop a categorization system for coding the content of the story. Share your content analysis with a friend who has not read the magazine. How much of the content of the story does your friend obtain from your content analysis? What does this suggest to you about the uses of content analysis?

8

Focus Groups in Practice

We have come a long way since focus groups were used in the evaluation of audience response to radio programs during the early 1940s (cf. Merton, 1987; Merton & Kendall, 1946). Focus groups are now widely used for a variety of purposes and in many different settings. Common uses of focus groups include obtaining general background information about a topic, generating research hypotheses, stimulating new ideas and creativity, generating impressions of products or programs, diagnosing the potential for problems, facilitating the interpretation of previously obtained quantitative results, and obtaining new insights and knowledge about phenomena of interest. Focus group settings range from well-equipped research laboratories to the casual, more relaxed surroundings of residences.

Before we illustrate some applications of focus groups, and in view of the five decades of "research tradition" of focus groups, we need to pause and ask ourselves the following questions:

- Has the conduct of focus groups changed over the years?
- Is focus group research more rigorous than it was 10 or 20 years ago?
- Do we have more confidence in the findings of focus group research in terms of its validity and usefulness as a result of 50 years of experience with the method?
- Do we have better trained and knowledgeable professionals to moderate focus groups than in the past? Do we have a better understanding of the role of the moderator and the factors that should be considered when selecting a moderator for a particular group?
- Are current facilities more conducive to focus group participation?
- Has the availability of information technology and the use of virtual focus groups enabled us to do better or different kinds of research?
- Do we have a better understanding of the dynamics of groups and the factors that can facilitate and limit participation and the quality of focus group data?
- Are the users of focus group research more aware of the purpose and strengths, as well as the limitations, of focus groups?

Insofar as science is a cumulative endeavor and focus group interviewing is a scientific method, the answers to all of these questions should be yes. Although it is undoubtedly true that there is a great deal of art in the actual practice of focus group research, this is true of the practice of all scientific methods. That there is a certain art to conducting focus groups or designing good experiments does not make these methods less scientific. The ultimate test of a method as a tool of science is its ability to produce sound and useful knowledge. By this test, one would have to consider focus group interviewing a well-established and rigorous tool of science. Thus, the answer to each of the questions posed above would be yes, but in most cases the answer would have to be qualified because focus group interviewing has been, and remains, one of the most widely abused of scientific tools (Nelems, 2003).

The abuse of the focus group interview is in large measure a result of its apparent ease and low cost, relative to other tools for social science research. This is, of course, an illusion because a properly designed focus group is not any easier or cheaper than a survey or experimental design and indeed may be more difficult in some situations.

Throughout this book we have emphasized the need for adequate preparation and empathy in conducting meaningful focus groups. We have also regularly appealed to the wealth of theory and research in group dynamics, social psychology, and clinical psychology to guide the preparation, conduct, and interpretation of focus group research. We not only have a repertoire of interviewing and analytical techniques but also a wealth of experience in the form of both case histories and theoretical literature in a variety of contexts to help improve the efficacy of focus groups as a research technique and increase the validity of focus group data. The higher levels of training and preparation required of the moderator, the increased sophistication of analytical tools applied to interpreting focus group data, and the availability of modern, well-equipped interviewing facilities have helped raise the standards of focus group research in general.

Misunderstanding of the basic purpose and design of focus groups, inadequate moderator training and preparation, contrived settings, and overzealous or inappropriate use of focus group results, among other things, undermine the integrity of focus group research. Focus groups are not a substitute for survey research or experimentation when these latter techniques are more appropriate for the research question. By the same token, a survey or experiment is not a substitute in those situations for which focus group interviewing is appropriate. Throughout this book, we have delineated the role of focus group research in the social sciences and have identified those types of research questions for which the focus group is appropriate. Problems arise when focus group interviewing is used for purposes for which it was never intended. Such abuse is not unique to the focus group interview; it is true of virtually all research techniques. Nevertheless, focus groups may be somewhat more vulnerable to abuse simply because they appear so easy to do; they are less structured than most other research tools, in terms of both their design and method of analysis; and they produce data that more readily lend themselves to impressionistic interpretation.

A greater frequency of abuse does not render an approach less scientific or less rigorous. It does urge the user to exercise greater caution and vigilance when designing, conducting, and interpreting the results of a focus group. At the same time, it would be very shortsighted to dismiss the use of focus group interviewing, or any other method, because it is abused.

In the remainder of this chapter, we illustrate the utility of focus group interviewing by providing several examples of its use. These examples are taken from several different domains in order to highlight the versatility of the method. One example is from the political domain; a second example is taken from the world of advertising; a third example considers a social policy issue, impulsivity and shoplifting. The last example deals with consumer perceptions of their experience as shoppers for a new automobile. This final example is longer than the others and is designed to provide an example of how a focus group report looks. The report presented in this chapter is an abbreviated version of the original, but it provides a general model for potential users of focus groups.

BUSH, KERRY, AND FOCUS GROUPS

Focus groups have come to play an important role in political campaigns. They are used to obtain impressions, attitudes, and responses to candidates and their positions. Such groups are also used to test theories about reactions of the public at large to positions of and actions by political candidates. The idea behind such testing is that if actions and communications designed on the basis of information obtained from a variety of sources do not play well with a small group that is relatively representative of the American population, however small, a need to reconsider those actions becomes apparent. Finally, focus groups may help identify and refine campaign themes and messages.

The news report reproduced in Table 8.1 illustrates how focus groups may be useful for identifying underlying strengths and vulnerabilities of candidates. Throughout much of the 2004 presidential campaign, polling appeared to suggest that John Kerry was running comfortably ahead of George W. Bush. Yet, despite such positive results from quantitative polls, more in-depth interviewing in focus groups and in surveys revealed significant vulnerabilities of candidate Kerry. Many voters did not connect with Kerry, and although he was widely credited with winning the several presidential debates, these debates did not seem to resolve the uncertainty and discomfort among voters reflected in these focus groups. Although quite a few of the details about the focus group

TABLE 8.1
Focus Group Has Trouble Connecting With Kerry

With only 6 weeks left before the election, Democratic challenger John Kerry is still struggling to define his identity for voters who insist they don't know him well enough to elect him president.

More evidence of the problem of connection and communication that has plagued Kerry throughout his candidacy emerged this week at a focus group organized by the nonpartisan Annenberg Public Policy Center of the University of Pennsylvania.

Under questioning by pollster Peter Hart, a dozen undecided Missouri voters admitted they were waiting for the presidential debates before they made their minds up about Kerry.

"These debates will be crucial for John Kerry, far more than for Bush, because people still don't know what he stands for," said John George, a Democratic-leaning independent. "The debates will give us an opportunity to find out."

President Bush did not escape criticism by the Democrats, Republicans and independents that included a teacher, a tax examiner, a sales analyst, and a computer technician, ranging in age from 36 to 66.

They voiced dissatisfaction with his failure to resolve the war in Iraq as well as a foreign policy that alienated allies. The group members were only mildly critical of the economic situation.

And the complaints were always tempered by acknowledgment and admiration of the president's leadership in the war on terrorism and his rallying of the nation after the terrorist attacks of September 11, 2001.

Wayne Fields, director of American Culture Studies at Washington University in St. Louis, said he was not surprised by the wariness of Missourians toward Kerry and would be surprised if the Democrat won the state.

"The GOP has been effective at putting Kerry off his stride," Fields said. "Bush has successfully projected the idea of how well he is known and he has defined himself through 9/11."

Hart suggested that the apparent failure of Kerry to gain the Missourians' confidence might reflect the success of the Bush campaign's drive to portray the Democrat as duplicitous and indecisive.

"Kerry has been defined by the Bush attacks and that may be why the debates have become so important," he said. Hart added that Kerry might still be rescued by a so-called "insight moment," suddenly and dramatically providing his needed link to the viewers, during the three debates.

SOURCE: From Dobbin, M., "Focus group has trouble connecting with Kerry," Sept. 23, 2004. Reprinted with permission of Scripps Howard News Service.

sessions are missing from the report, it can be surmised that these groups were planned and implemented in a fairly systematic process, similar to one suggested in Figure 3.1 in Chapter 3.

TELEVISION ADS THE PUBLIC WILL NEVER SEE

From the reports on the president's desk in the Oval Office to the desks of CEOs of corporate giants like GE and AT&T, focus group research has provided the kind of insights that have prevented costly oversights and mistakes that might have led to foreign policy blunders and dinosaur advertising campaigns.

Although more than $63 billion was spent on television advertising in the United States in 2004, this figure hides the fact that a surprising number of commercials costing millions of dollars never made it to the television screens. Many of these costly commercials were scrapped or cancelled, even after companies had already spent a great deal of time and money on their production and prelaunch testing. Despite the time and expense that go into the making and testing of commercials, corporations do not hesitate to axe those ads that do not cut it because it is far better to write off $200,000 on production costs than to spend $20 million on an advertising campaign that does not work. Properly timed and executed focus groups can reduce or eliminate the expense that goes into producing and filming a commercial. Such groups can be very helpful in determining what messages are important and effective. Focus groups can also suggest ways to improve commercials by identifying points of confusion, better wording, or stronger visuals.

IMPULSIVE CONSUMERS, SHOPLIFTERS, AND FOCUS GROUPS

Focus groups are particularly useful for investigating topics that are considered to be sensitive and socially undesirable, such as the reasons why consumers give in to their impulses to buy or the reasons why people shoplift. When investigating such topics, focus groups provide a facilitating effect for eliciting consumer motivations and circumstances behind their actions, which are not found in either phone or personal interviews or even in anonymous surveys. The admission by other group members that they too have a problem or engage in certain behaviors often legitimizes discussions and provides a level of candor not found in other settings. Using focus groups for such research objectives is not only more efficient, but it may be the only means for eliciting motivations that underlie behavior. With some warm-up, presession briefing, and clever moderating, it is possible for any group of people to talk openly about their experiences. Sometimes the group, through a shared sense of experiences (both positive and negative), can enhance the breadth and depth of discussion beyond that obtained in personal interviews.

Focus groups may be more effective than telephone interviews, given the sense of impersonality and insecurity that often accompany answering questions to strangers over the phone. Surveys have the advantage of preserving respondent anonymity but fall short in offering depth of discussion that can only come about through probing and clarifying. Furthermore, as noted in earlier chapters, the anonymity barrier may be easily broken down through certain warm-up and interviewing strategies that make the participants more at ease about relating their experiences.

In a focus group investigating students' attitudes toward shoplifting, it was discovered that it was fairly easy to get students to talk openly about their attitudes, as well as their shoplifting experiences. A mere demonstration of empathy and willingness to learn was sufficient to elicit focus group participants' motivations for shoplifting. In comparison, when conducting a group of in-depth interviews on impulse buying, it was often difficult to break down the rationality or defensive element in respondents' recollections of their impulsive experiences. Pacification strategies such as reminding respondents that "there is nothing irrational about buying something on impulse" and "I am sure most of us have bought one thing or another on impulse before" were often used in the in-depth interviews to facilitate discussion of impulsive tendencies.

Focus groups could have offered a much more efficient and less time-consuming way of probing consumers' impulsive tendencies, first by starting the focus group session with a personal anecdote and, second, by adopting a nonjudgmental moderating style. Additionally, in such situations, focus group participants tend to feel more relaxed as they feed off each other's experiences and find that they are not being isolated for in-depth scrutiny as would be the case with personal interviews. This experience highlights the effectiveness of using focus groups for probing consumers' sensitive experiences.

A REPRESENTATIVE FOCUS GROUP REPORT: BUYING A NEW CAR

In order to provide some sense of what a focus group report looks like, the following representative report is included in this chapter. As we noted at the beginning of the chapter, this report is somewhat abbreviated and includes only a descriptive analysis. Nevertheless, it should provide a useful illustration for anyone contemplating writing such a report. The report deals with a topic with which many individuals can identify, the purchase of a new automobile. The report summarizes four focus groups carried out for a major automobile manufacturer who was interested in learning something about the shopping experiences of consumers within a particular metropolitan area. This manufacturer had a special interest in how dealerships in the area performed and how consumers viewed their experiences with dealerships. Much of the discussion dealing with the manufacturer's own dealerships has been eliminated.

NEW CAR PURCHASING EXPERIENCES: A SAMPLE REPORT

Purpose

Four focus groups were carried out in a major metropolitan area for the purpose of exploring the experiences, perceptions, and attitudes of new car purchasers in the area. Members of the groups were asked to discuss the factors that influenced their most recent car purchase, the perceptions of competing makes and models, and the types of shopping activities in which they engaged. They were also asked to discuss their experience with the new car after the sale, including their service needs and overall satisfaction with the automobile. A copy of the interview guide is provided in Table 8.2.

Composition of the Groups

The groups were composed of 9 to 12 individuals who had purchased a new passenger vehicle within the past 12 months. Participants were selected randomly from a list of new car registrants as compiled by R. L. Polk and Company, which uses vehicle registration information supplied by state motor vehicle bureaus. This random selection procedure ensured a mix of ages, income levels, and type of vehicle purchased. Individuals who worked for a local automobile dealership or had an immediate family member who did were excluded from participation. All participants were either the primary decision maker in the vehicle purchase or the primary user of the vehicle. All participants were compensated for participation. Two locations were selected to provide some geographic diversity to the groups. All groups lasted approximately 90 minutes.

Major Factors Influencing Vehicle Purchase

Each group discussion began with consideration of the factors that are influential in the purchase of the automobile. Participants were given the opportunity to volunteer the specific factors most important in their own decision.

TABLE 8.2
Interview Guide for New Car Purchasers

1. All of you here recently purchased new automobiles. As a way to get started, let's talk about the factors that influenced your decision to buy the car that you purchased. [If not raised by the group, probe for the importance of each of the following:]
   a. Dealership, including the specific location of the dealership
   b. Sales personnel
   c. Friends, relatives, or other significant individuals
   d. Prior experience with make or model or with dealer
   e. Type of vehicle desired and purpose it would serve
   f. Service expectations
   g. Deals (special prices or packages, special financing, trade-in allowances, etc.)
   h. Price
   i. Advertising

2. Let's discuss how you feel about the experience. Was it a pleasant or unpleasant experience?
   [Probe: Why? What factors were most important in making the experience positive or negative?]

3. If you could change the purchasing experience in any way, what would you change?
   [Probe: Why? Why would this change make a difference?]

4. Do you feel you got a good deal in your last purchase?
   [Probe: Why or why not? What makes you think this?]

5. Some of you bought American automobiles, and others bought foreign cars. Do you see any differences in the process of buying American versus foreign-made cars?
   [Probe: Why do you think these differences exist?]

6. Have any of you had contact with the dealer or salesperson since you bought the car?
   [Probe: What kind of contact? Was this contact pleasant or unpleasant? Why?]

7. What do you expect of an automobile dealer during and after the sale?
   [Probe: How many of you feel these expectations have been met by your dealer?]

8. Is there anything else about your purchase experience that you would like to share that we have not yet touched upon?

Other specific factors were offered by the moderator for discussion by the group if they were not spontaneously identified by members of the group. Among the factors raised by the moderator were the dealership (including the specific location of the dealership), prior experiences with various vehicles, the specific type of vehicle desired, service expectations, and deals offered.

Members of the groups offered a wide variety of opinions regarding the relative importance of various factors that influenced their purchase. Price appeared to be uniformly important in the purchase decision, but participants differed as to whether sticker price, monthly note, price less trade-in, or some combination of these factors was most important. In general, it appeared that these new car purchasers selected a general type of vehicle (and in some cases, a specific make and model), then sought an acceptable deal. Despite the perceived importance of price, the degree of price shopping and comparison of deals varied widely across participants. Most of the participants appeared to have obtained an acceptable deal. Despite the perceived importance of price, the degree of price shopping and comparison of deals varied widely across participants. Most of the participants appeared to have a reference price for the automobile they were seeking. Some of these reference prices were obtained by comparing deals offered at competing dealerships. Reference prices were also obtained from *Consumer Reports* or from online sources by a number of the participants. Among the comments regarding the importance of price were the following:

It is everything. It's the most important thing.

Monthly note was most important to me. I needed to be sure I could afford the notes.

A number of participants expressed frustration with the process of obtaining a firm price, and others reported difficulty in determining the bottom line after such factors as option packages and trade-in were factored into the price. This was not a uniform problem for all respondents, but among those who reported experiencing it, the problem was the source of considerable displeasure and often resulted in their taking their business elsewhere. Among the statements regarding this problem were the following:

Why can't they just tell you the price?

Why do they always have to go to the sales manager to check the price? They ought to be able to quote a price without making you wait.

It's just a game they play to make you anxious. They shouldn't play games.

There was much suspicion among the participants that salespeople never provided the actual dealer cost to the buyer. Rather, there was considerable sentiment that the invoice the buyer is shown is not an accurate reflection of dealer cost:

The invoice they show you is not what they really pay for the car.

Financing was frequently mentioned as an important reason for having bought a particular make. Many of the participants had taken advantage of special low-rate dealer or manufacturer financing. The importance of financing was revealed in a variety of statements:

I've always bought Ford before, but they turned me down for financing.

They offered 3.2% financing, so I bought.

The importance of the dealership in the purchase decision varied considerably among the participants. Members of the groups for whom price was the most important factor did not place much emphasis on the location or characteristics of the dealership:

I was looking for the lowest price.

I figure I can get the car serviced anywhere, so I bought where they gave me the best deal.

On the other hand, there were a number of participants for whom the dealership was very important. These individuals either were concerned about service after the sale and desired to do business with a dealer in a convenient location, or they had previous positive experiences with a particular dealership:

I wanted a convenient place to take my car for service.

I have always gotten good service from Jones, so I always go there.

There was general agreement among all the respondents that their loyalty to a particular dealership was limited. Even with a positive prior experience at a particular dealership, respondents indicated that they typically shopped around. In most cases, a positive previous experience was sufficient for the dealership to be contacted the next time a purchase was planned, but it was insufficient reason to buy:

It's such a big investment now. You have to shop around.

I'd go back again, but if they didn't offer me a good deal I'd go someplace else.

I bought from Wilson because he always treats me right, but you have to look around.

Advertising appeared to play a very limited role in the purchases of the group members. Many individuals reported that they looked at prices and financing advertised in the paper, and a few individuals reported using magazine and television advertising to obtain information about styling. Advertising appeared to be used for information very early in the search process. Advertising played a major role in creating consumer awareness and willingness to consider particular makes and models but did not appear to be a strong factor in the purchase decision itself. On the other hand, the salesperson with whom the participants dealt was perceived to be quite critical to the purchase decision. Participants reported a wide variety of experiences with sales personnel and made it quite clear that their treatment by sales personnel was influential in their purchase. Aggressive, pushy salespeople were uniformly disliked, but so were nonchalant and indifferent sales personnel. For these respondents, there appeared to be an optimal level of sales assistance that was perceived as helpful without being pushy.

Participants felt that the sales personnel with whom they had positive experiences were able to provide information about the cars they sold and would work with the buyer to determine price, financing, and options packages. They did not like sales personnel who attacked them as they came on the lot. Neither did they like being followed about by sales personnel. Sales personnel who could not or would not answer questions about particular makes were perceived in a very negative light. Representative comments concerning sales personnel include the following:

She knew everything about the car and could answer all my questions. She wasn't pushy, but she really worked with me (from a male participant).

He wouldn't even let me sit in the cars. . . . He really made me mad.

He wasn't pushy. He worked with me and answered my questions.

A good salesman ought to know about the car he's selling. He ought to be able to explain things.

He kept telling me what I should buy and not buy. He cut his nose off to spite his face.

He wouldn't talk to me. I wanted him to tell me about the car. He seemed to take the attitude that I could buy if I wanted to.

About half of the participants reported that the salesperson had been in touch with them since the purchase. Some had received telephone calls, letters, or Christmas cards. In a few cases, the salesperson had assisted with service problems that had occurred. Virtually all of the respondents indicated that they appreciated this contact and indicated it would probably make them consider the salesperson or dealership the next time that they purchased. They also indicated, however, that such contact would be insufficient reason to purchase from the salesperson on the next purchase occasion:

Sure it's nice, and I'll probably consider the dealer the next time I buy, but he'll still have to offer me a good deal.

A number of participants noted a difference between import and domestic dealers:

The import salesman is more like an order taker. You have to wait to get the car, so they really don't have to sell you.

Several of the participants indicated that the salesperson had introduced them to the service department at the time of the sale. Most participants felt this was important, and several remarked that they wish their salesperson had done so. This was perceived as unimportant only by participants who were already acquainted with service personnel or who had no plans to have their car serviced at the dealership.

Friends and acquaintances were important in the purchase process of virtually all of the participants, but their role varied. Friends were a common source of information about the reputation of a car and dealership. In some cases, friends or relatives had accompanied the purchaser to the showroom to assist in the purchase. This appeared to be more often the case among the women purchasers, and the response of the salesperson to this "purchase pal" often influenced the outcome of the sale:

He answered my questions. It was my truck, not my fiancé's, so he talked to me.

I got so mad. He wouldn't talk to me, and I was the one buying the car. I didn't buy from him.

Warranty and service after the sale were important to a substantial subset of the participants. Extended warranties were mentioned as important factors in the purchase decision of a number of participants. Several participants reported that they returned to dealerships from which they had bought previously because of their positive experiences with the service department. Others indicated that they had not returned to a particular dealership because of problems with service on previous cars:

I have bought from three different Ford dealers, and none of them provided good service, so I won't buy a Ford.

We had an experience that could have been terrible, . . . a car that we had a lot of trouble with, but the dealer stood behind it. When we bought again we went back to that dealer.

The automobile itself was reported to be quite important in the purchase process, and most respondents had a particular model or set of models in mind prior to beginning the purchase process. Many of the participants reported consulting friends and publications such as *Consumer Reports*. Participants who changed their minds and bought a car outside of the original set indicated that they did so because of an unpleasant experience in the purchase process or because they discovered another model in the course of their search.

Few participants regarded the purchase process as unpleasant, but many did feel that it was unnecessarily complex. These individuals complained of being unable to easily obtain information, of being unable to obtain a firm purchase price, or being unable to identify a fair price. There was also considerable objection to the salesperson being unable to make a deal without consulting with the sales manager. Most respondents wanted a simpler, more straightforward shopping experience. Several commented that it should be like retail shopping where the price is posted and you buy off the shelf. The negotiation process appeared to be a source of discomfort and/or irritation to a number of the participants. Women participants were particularly likely to report that the experience was traumatic:

It makes me sick to my stomach every time I go in.

I do a thing up front with them. I tell them they aren't going to take advantage of me just because I am a woman.

Participants reported a range of experiences with service after the sale. All participants had strong views about what would constitute acceptable service:

They ought to fix the problem the first time. I shouldn't have to take it back for the same problem.

They should be willing to answer questions. I ought to be able to call if the car doesn't sound right and get an answer about whether it should sound that way.

I expect them to be prompt. If they tell me to be there at 7:00 A.M., they should be ready for me at 7. I shouldn't get there with 20 other people and have to wait.

They should honor the warranty, and they should provide a car.

A dealer shouldn't have to order a part; they ought to have parts in stock.

They're too expensive. If I bought my car from them, they shouldn't charge me more than a shade-tree mechanic.

Participants felt very strongly that the dealer had an obligation to provide timely service with a minimum of inconvenience. If the car was under warranty, they felt the dealer should provide alternative transportation. Several participants felt that dealers should provide free or inexpensive rental cars, even when the car was no longer under warranty, as a gesture of goodwill:

If they want me to come back, they ought to provide a car.

There was a general perception that service costs are too high, particularly for minor items:

I had to have a hubcap snapped back on, and they charged me $30. Imagine what they do to you on a big job!

The expertise of service departments was questioned by several participants:

I'd rather take my car to a specialist. If I have a transmission problem, I'd rather take it to a transmission place that does transmissions all the time. And they're cheaper.

They couldn't solve the problem . . . because they're just plain stupid.

Members of all the groups expressed a near consensus that a service department should make appointments for routine work and should honor those appointments. They felt that work should be explained to them and that when a commitment is made to complete work by a specified time, that commitment should be met. They felt the car should be returned clean and free from dirt and grease.

There was a strong sense among the participants that their purchase of an automobile from a dealer created an obligation to provide service over and beyond that provided a nonpurchaser. They felt that purchasers should be given priority treatment.

Service seemed to be a sore point for many of the participants. For some, there was a sense that American automobiles required too much service to begin with, so service should be prompt and convenient.

Participants in the groups uniformly agreed that import automobiles are superior to American automobiles in dependability, styling, and workmanship. Older participants suggested that the quality of American cars began to deteriorate in the early 1970s when a shift to smaller, more efficient automobiles was caused by the energy crisis. Most participants agreed that the quality of American automobiles has improved in recent years, but they still perceive imports as superior. Several of the import owners suggested that the durability and reliability of imports were the reasons for their purchase. This perceived superiority was strong enough to lead purchasers to wait for the delivery of their new automobiles. Virtually all of the import purchasers reported having ordered their cars and waiting 1 to 2 months for delivery.

In addition to the perception of poorer mechanical reliability, participants suggested that the quality of ride offered by imports was superior. They suggested that American cars felt light and hollow, did not handle as well, and offered less comfort. In addition, several participants criticized the styling of American automobiles:

They all look alike. They are too concerned with aerodynamics. I don't like the way they look.

They don't spend enough time on design.

The group members did generally agree that Americans make good large cars, and those participants who had bought American cars frequently indicated that they were looking for a larger car.

Even among those participants who believed that they should buy American, there was resentment of being made to feel guilty about buying an import. Participants suggested they would buy more American cars when quality improved. They indicated they would use the experience of friends and the reports of such publications as *Consumer Reports* to determine whether the quality of American automobiles had improved. Several respondents also observed that it had become increasingly difficult to determine what was really an "American" car.

Summary

Members of four focus groups reported their experiences in purchasing a new passenger vehicle. These experiences ranged from very positive to very negative. In general, positive purchasing experiences were associated with a helpful and informative salesperson who did not employ high-pressure sales tactics. Purchasers reported that they appreciated salespeople who were knowledgeable about the products they sold, volunteered information, and answered questions readily and directly. They were put off by salespeople who were either pushy or nonchalant and salespeople who either tried to tell them what to buy or were not direct in answering questions.

Although price, product, dealership, and service were all mentioned as important reasons for a purchase, the attitudes and approach of the salesperson appear to have been a primary factor in the final purchase decision.

Service was an important factor in the purchase of many but not all the participants. Indeed, where an individual was a repeat purchaser from the same dealership, the service they had received on a previous car appeared to be the primary reason for the repeat purchase. On the other hand, numerous participants stated they were price shoppers who were looking for the best deal. For these individuals, service was not a primary consideration when deciding whether to purchase from a particular dealer. Participants generally felt that service should be prompt and done right the first time. They felt that when a car is under warranty, they are entitled to alternate transportation when the car is being serviced.

American automobiles are evaluated less positively than their imported counterparts. This perceived difference is sufficiently strong that a number of the purchasers were willing to wait several months for an import to be delivered. Salespeople at import dealerships were perceived more as order takers than someone trying to make a sale. Thus, they were regarded as less helpful but, at the same time, less pushy than salespeople at dealerships that carried American-made automobiles.

CONCLUSION

Chapter 8 provides examples of the use of focus groups for several different purposes. It provides an illustration of the use of focus groups to test hypotheses and several other more exploratory applications. The chapter also provides an extended example of one application that includes a representative report.

REVIEW QUESTIONS

1. Focus groups are often considered to be most appropriate for exploratory research. Yet, the examples in this chapter also suggest that focus groups may also be used for evaluation. What is the role of group research in evaluation and decision making?

2. Why are focus groups often used to evaluate advertisements? What information does a focus group interview provide that could not be obtained in a survey or an experiment designed to measure the effect of an ad?

3. Earlier in the book, it was suggested that focus groups could be used even for sensitive topics. One of the illustrations given in the chapter deals with a discussion of an activity, shoplifting, which is a criminal offense. Why do you think people are willing to discuss such activities in a group setting? Do you see any ethical dilemma for the researcher in this example?

4. Critique the interview guide used in the car-buying illustration. Revise the guide in a fashion that resolves any criticism you have of the guide used.

5. What additional types of analyses might have been carried out in the car-buying illustration? Under what circumstances might these additional analyses be justified?

Exercise: Reread the focus group report on automobile purchasing. If you were a new car manufacturer, what actions might you take based on this report? What type(s) of further research might you pursue? How would the results of the focus group interviews assist you in designing this additional research?

9

Other Group Methods

Focus groups are but one of a number of research techniques that involve the use of groups. Although most of this book is concerned with focus groups, much of the discussion is applicable to the other techniques. In addition, there are circumstances and research questions for which group techniques other than traditional focus groups may be more appropriate. For these reasons, we will identify and briefly discuss five other group techniques: the nominal group technique, the Delphi technique, brainstorming, synectics, and leaderless discussion groups.

THE NOMINAL GROUP TECHNIQUE

An alternative approach to group interviewing has come to be called the nominal group technique (NGT). Nominal groups are groups in name only. The participants may not even meet. Even when they do meet, they do not directly interact with one another, at least in the early stages of the meeting. Rather, each member of the group is interviewed as an individual, and summaries of the responses and ideas of other group members are provided to the other members. Nominal groups may be useful when it is not possible to assemble a particular group of interest on a timely basis. This is often the case with very specialized groups like scientists, very senior business executives, and high-level government officials. In such cases, the researcher may obtain a first round of responses from each member of the group, summarize the responses, share the summary (in greater or lesser detail) with members of the group, then ask for a second round of responses. Alternatively, the members of the group may be brought together, but they are asked to speak one at a time in response to questions. Thus, participants may hear the answers of other group members and elaborate on them when it is their turn, but they are not allowed to interact spontaneously.

An even more common reason for using the nominal group technique is to avoid the influence of group opinion or the opinions of one or more very dominant group members on the responses of individuals. Although the opportunities for group synergy and facilitation of response are important advantages of focus groups, there are some circumstances in which the group setting may inhibit the responsiveness of the group as a whole or of some individual members of the group. This may happen when the group to be interviewed includes supervisors and subordinates, parents and their children, an individual member who is recognized by other members as having unusual expertise on the topic to be discussed, or an individual with a particularly dominant personality. The nominal group technique may also be appropriate when there is reason to believe that the level of conflict among group members is sufficiently great that it interferes with discussion of the topic of interest. Finally, the nominal group technique may be useful even when the majority of group members share the same general opinions. A strong majority opinion, or even a strong plurality, may inhibit the responses of members of the groups who hold dissenting opinions.

Sometimes the nominal group technique is combined with a more traditional focus group to obtain the best features of both. In these cases, a nominal group technique is used to obtain the independent responses of individuals. Summaries of these responses are distributed to members of the group before or during the group discussion. The preliminary nominal group exercise ensures that all opinions are adequately represented and provides input for the focus group discussion. A more detailed discussion of the nominal group technique as well as examples of its use may be found in Delbecq, Van de Ven, and Gustafson (1975) and Moore (1987) in this series of Sage publications.

THE DELPHI TECHNIQUE

A specialized application of the nominal group technique is used for purposes of developing forecasts of future events and trends based on the collective opinion of knowledgeable experts. The technique derives its name from the oracle of Delphi in ancient Greece. The oracle was reputed to be able to see the future. Many forecasting problems cannot be solved with quantitative tools because the historical data on which these techniques depend is unavailable or the data that are available provide little or no insight into the probability of events of interest. This is often the case when forecasts of long-term social trends or technological developments are of interest or when there is a need to forecast the timing of an infrequent event or the implications of a new-to-the-world social or product innovation.

One area of research that is particularly well suited for research using the Delphi technique is the impact of new technology. In areas such as information and telecommunications, technological advances can have profound implications for lifestyles (e.g., the growth of telecommuting), for legislation and regulation (e.g., the telephone company now finds itself competing with its customers in offering certain types of services and it is no longer so clear who needs regulation), in the way business is done (computer-aided manufacturing is radically altering the traditional assembly line), and in personnel requirements of organizations (computer literacy is necessary for many of the jobs being created today). Dealing with changes in technology and its implications is difficult, but forecasting what new technologies will be available at a given point in time and what the implications will be is even more difficult. There are no mathematical algorithms to turn to for guidance.

Indeed, this type of problem is extremely complex. There is a need to understand where technology will be at any one point in time. Predicting the advance of technology, which tends to be discontinuous and nonlinear, is itself difficult. Then predicting the impact of the technology is even more difficult. Putting technological forecasts together with forecasts of the implications of technology is an extraordinarily difficult task but one that is essential for a large number of organizations. The Delphi technique represents one approach to the solution of this problem.

The Delphi technique requires a panel of experts on the social or technological trends of interest. Members of this panel are asked to provide independent forecasts of events they expect to occur and to identify the assumptions on which they base their forecasts. Such forecasts may include estimates of whether particular events or scenarios will occur, or they may include specific point estimates, such as the rate of inflation in the third quarter of next year. These experts may also be asked to provide ranges or confidence intervals associated with their forecasts, particularly when specific point estimates are involved. These independent forecasts are summarized in statistical form and key assumptions identified. These summaries and assumptions are provided to all members of the panel, and each member is asked to provide a new forecast based on this new information. These new forecasts are summarized and reported to the panel members, who are again asked to revise their forecasts. This iterative process continues until a consensus is obtained or no further changes occur in the individual forecasts. In practice, it has been observed that the Delphi technique seldom requires more than three or four iterations. Figure 9.1 illustrates the steps in the process.

The critical elements of the Delphi technique are the identification of the panel of experts, the design of the set of questions used to elicit forecasts and assumptions, and the summarization of the individual input. Although the group does not meet face to face, the facilitators of a Delphi exercise play a critical role because they control these key elements. More detailed discussions of the Delphi technique may be found in Dalkey and Helmer (1963), Linstone and Turoff (1975), and Moore (1987) in this series.

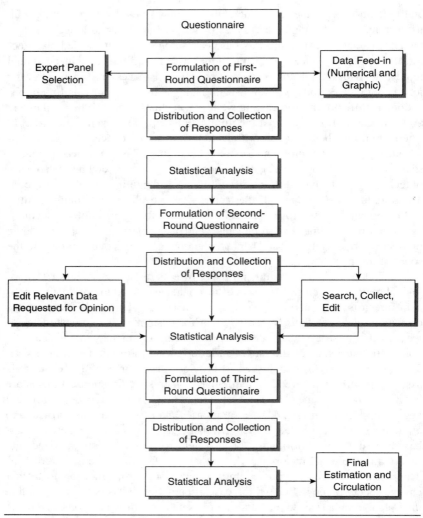

Figure 9.1   Flowchart of Delphi Technique

BRAINSTORMING AND SYNECTICS

Although brainstorming and synectics are rather different techniques, both are group techniques that are designed to facilitate the generation of new ideas and encourage creative expression. Traditional brainstorming sessions involve groups who may or may not have a designated moderator. Group members are instructed to generate ideas, approaches, or solutions without regard to cost, practicality, or feasibility. Members of the group are not to be critical of any ideas generated by others. Instead, they are encouraged to build on the ideas of others by suggesting embellishments, improvements, and modifications.

Brainstorming can be an exciting, creative experience. The emphasis of the exercise is on the quantity of ideas produced because the greater the number of ideas generated, the higher the probability that at least some will be good ideas. It should be pointed out, however, that brainstorming appears to be most useful for problems that have no single best solution and when the interaction and different perspectives of group members facilitate creativity.

Some focus groups often resemble a brainstorming session. For example, it is quite common for manufacturing and service firms to bring together customers and potential customers to talk about new products, product modifications, or problems for which a new product might be useful.

Synectics is a somewhat more structured approach to the generation of ideas. A trained moderator generally leads a synectics group and tries to get the group to view problems, needs, or actions from new and often unusual perspectives. For example, the moderator may suggest that the group is stranded on a desert island with none of the traditional tools to accomplish some simple tasks; there are, however, ample natural resources. A related example would involve the group being told that the space shuttle just crashed on an unknown island with no means to communicate to the outside world. The group might be asked to think of all the ways the technology in the shuttle could be used to help the occupants survive. The outcome of such an exercise could be the identification of new commercial opportunities for technologies developed in the space program.

The role of the moderator in a synectics session is to use a variety of techniques to simultaneously create the noncritical and accepting atmosphere that characterizes a brainstorming session and to force participants out of habitual perceptual and problem-solving modes and into more creative and innovative modes of analysis. Synectics has been rather widely used in business organizations as a means for generating ideas for new products and services. There are five basic principles underlying the synectics approach:

1. *Deferment,* that is, look first for viewpoints or perspectives, rather than solutions. For example, rather than immediately discussing the types of pumps available for moving water, a synectics groups might discuss the more general problem of how to move "things" from one place to another.

2. *Autonomy* of the object, that is, let the problem take on a life of its own. For example, instead of talking about what is feasible with respect to the design

of software for desktop publishing, the group might focus on what would be
an ideal desktop publishing system. Thus, the problem rather than potential
solutions becomes the focus of the discussion.

3. *Use of the commonplace,* that is, try to use the familiar as a way of gaining
   perspective on the strange. An example of this approach would be a university
   faculty group given the task of designing a curriculum in computer science for
   incoming freshmen. Rather than focus on the unfamiliar—computer science—
   the group might be asked to focus on what would constitute mastery of an area
   within the curriculum.

4. *Involvement/detachment,* that is, alternating between the general and the specific so that specific instances may be identified and seen as part of a larger
   perspective.

5. *Use of metaphor,* that is, use analogies to suggest new viewpoints. (Osborn,
   1963, p. 274)

Among the techniques that a synectics moderator might use to facilitate
creativity are moving from the most general to the most specific example of
a problem or process (or vice versa), the use of role playing, and discovery
of analogies. When individuals or groups immediately focus on a very specific issue, there is frequently a rapid narrowing of perspective that occurs
because people tend to use their prior experience and past solutions as a
point of reference. Thus, a group of engineers asked to consider new designs
for pumping equipment tends to think of the way pumps have been designed
in the past. Changing perspective by considering a more general problem,
such as how one might move a liquid from one place to another, may facilitate the identification of radical new designs that have little in common with
past designs.

Role playing may also help change perspectives. For example, a group of
architects might be told to pretend they are a wall and describe how they feel
and how they relate to other parts of the building. Analogies may serve a similar purpose. When analogies are used in a synectics session, the group
members are instructed to come up with ideas that are similar but not identical to some reference object. Table 9.1 summarizes a number of techniques
that may be employed in a synectics session.

Brainstorming and synectics are but two of numerous group techniques that
have been developed to facilitate creativity and the generation of ideas. A more
thorough treatment of brainstorming and synectics, as well as other group creativity techniques, may be found in Arnold (1962) and Osborn (1963).

TABLE 9.1
Techniques Used to Facilitate Creativity in Synectics Groups

Technique	Description
Personal analogy	Participant puts himself in the place of a physical object (e.g., a tuning fork, a wall, or a product) and gives a first-person description of what it feels like to be that object.
Book title	Participant gives a two-word phrase that captures the essence and paradox involved in a particular thing or set of feelings (e.g., familiar surprise, interested disbelief).
Example excursion	Group discusses a topic seemingly unrelated to the basic problem in order to trigger thoughts and/or "take a vacation" from the problem.
Force fit–get fired	Participant thinks of an idea to force together two or more components of an idea. In the get-fired technique, the idea is to be so wild that his boss will fire him.

LEADERLESS DISCUSSION GROUPS

There are occasions when interest in the content of a group discussion is of less importance than the dynamics of the group itself. Communication patterns among group members, the actions of individual group members, and even the alliances or coalitions that form in a group may be of interest to a researcher. This is particularly true in personnel assessment situations when interpersonal skills need to be evaluated. Leadership discussion groups provide an approach to this type of assessment and research. For example, a trait that is highly desirable in certain types of managers is the ability to facilitate action toward a common goal among individuals who do not directly report to the manager. Product managers in marketing organizations often have responsibility for coordinating a team of individuals over whom they have no direct responsibility. A leaderless discussion group provides one vehicle for assessing the extent to which an individual can give direction and obtain results in such situations.

Leaderless discussion groups are well described by their name. There is no moderator or leader designated for the group. The group is given instructions, which may range from a general and ambiguous task like, "Do something productive with your time during the next 90 minutes," to a very specific task such as producing a product or report. The group is observed as it completes the task, and the patterns of interaction among members are recorded. Some members of the group tend to emerge as more dominant than others. One or more individuals may assume a leadership role, and other members of the group may assume other roles, such as peacemaker, arbiter, or cheerleader.

Leaderless discussion groups are widely used as assessment tools in organizations, particularly for management positions and positions involving personal selling activities. There is a rich and large literature on the use of leaderless discussion groups. Stogdill and Coons (1957) and Finkle (1976) provide a useful introduction to this literature.

As we have seen, focus groups are but one type of research technique involving the use of groups. Although focus groups are very flexible, there may be occasions when one of these other techniques, such as those discussed briefly above, is more appropriate. The reader interested in using other group techniques should consult sources that emphasize these techniques and the unique issues and problems associated with their use.

CONCLUSION

Focus group research is a useful research tool, but there are many other tools in the toolbox. It is important to recognize the unique strengths and limitations of focus group research. Focus group research produces very specific types of data that are at once very rich and diagnostic and limited. The use of focus groups can produce powerful insights, but such use is not a substitute for other research techniques.

REVIEW QUESTIONS

1. How do focus groups differ from other group techniques such as the nominal group technique, synectics, leaderless discussion groups, and the Delphi technique?

2. Consider a research project that will use the Delphi technique to predict food consumption trends in the United States 10 years from now. What experts from which fields would you select to participate, and why?

3. Imagine you are designing a synectics project to generate ideas for the design of the next generation of cell phones. What metaphors would you employ to better understand consumers' cell phone relationships, gratifications, and frustrations? For example, "If my cell phone were a _____ (person, object, animal, tree, etc.), it would be a _____." Repeat several times.

4. Which of the following issues would best be addressed with the nominal group technique and why?

   Assessing consumers' attitudes about potato chips

   Understanding doctors' and nurses' working relationships

   Generating ideas for improving customer service in pharmacies

5. In conducting brainstorming sessions, a core principle prohibits any critical evaluation of ideas that are expressed in the group. This is often easier said than done. What rules or sanctions would you use to discourage participants from expressing negative, critical comments?

Exercise: Organize and lead either a leaderless discussion group or a nominal group. You can keep the discussion to 30 minutes. How does the discussion differ from that of a focus group? If you conducted a leaderless discussion group, what did this exercise suggest about the role of a moderator in a focus group? If you conducted a nominal group, what did this exercise suggest about the role of group interaction in a focus group?

10

Conclusion

Focus groups are among the more common forms of research in a wide array of disciplines. They are used by academic researchers, government policy makers, and business decision makers. Focus groups provide a rich and detailed set of data about perceptions, thoughts, feelings, and impressions of group members in the members' own words. They represent a remarkably flexible research tool in that they can be adapted to obtain information about almost any topic, in a wide array of settings, and from very different types of individuals. Group discussions may be quite general or very specific; they may be highly structured or quite unstructured. Visual stimuli, demonstrations, or other activities may be used within the context of a focus group in order to provide a basis for discussion. This flexibility makes the focus group a particularly useful tool and explains its popularity.

The decision to use a focus group or some other research tool must be based on the appropriateness of the method for obtaining answers to specific research questions. It has been said that to a man with a hammer, everything is a nail. All too often researchers are like the man with a hammer; one method or technique becomes the means by which all research problems are addressed, and other methods are either ignored or discounted. So it has been with focus group interviewing. For other researchers, focus groups are never appropriate. The truth lies somewhere in the middle. Focus groups are useful for particular purposes and specific situations, for exploring the way particular groups of individuals think and talk about a phenomenon, for generating ideas, and for generating diagnostic information. For these purposes, focus groups represent a rigorous scientific method of inquiry.

Focus groups are not the most appropriate means for obtaining an estimate of a parameter of a population with a small band of confidence. Neither are they the most appropriate tool for exploring the effect of an intervention on thoughts or behavior. On the other hand, descriptive survey data are not particularly useful for this latter purpose either unless they are obtained in the context of an experimental design. Survey data do not, as a rule, identify important qualifiers or contingencies that may be associated with an answer to a structured question, nor do they offer an opportunity for feedback from and response to the comments of others. Focus groups are more useful for these latter purposes.

The spontaneous interaction of focus group members often produces insights that are not readily, if ever, obtained in individual surveys or experiments. Surveys and experiments tend to provide feedback about the world or a specific phenomenon, as conceptualized by the researcher. This etic approach is quite useful, but it must be recognized that such conceptualizations may be at variance with the way individual respondents conceptualize the world. Focus groups are designed to help understand how individuals conceptualize and categorize a phenomenon. As such, the data generated by focus groups is more emic than etic.

Much of the power of the focus group as a method of inquiry grows out of the spontaneity and synergy of the group dynamic. Although it may be somewhat idiosyncratic and group specific, there are few areas in the social sciences that have been as carefully and intensively studied as the dynamics of small groups. Chapter 2 provided a review of this voluminous literature and drew implications for the design and conduct of focus groups from it. This literature makes obvious the fact that much is known about how groups behave and how groups may be managed to produce a particular outcome. Likewise, Chapter 5 reviewed the literature on interviewing and interviewer characteristics, made plain the basis for interviewer selection and training, and examined the influence of the interviewer on the group. The purpose of these chapters was to show the solid and extensive foundation on which group interviewing is based. Although it is undoubtedly true that there is a great deal of art involved in the moderation of focus groups, there is also a firm scientific base on which the method rests. Finally, Chapter 7 suggested that the analysis and interpretation of data generated by a focus group need not be subjective and impressionistic. Rather, such data are amenable to objective analysis that may range from simple qualitative description to complex quantitative analysis of cognitive networks.

One purpose of this book is to demonstrate that focus group research need not be subjective or lacking in rigor. Indeed, the focus group interview rests on an extensive body of empirical research and theory, as well as practice. It is not appropriate for all research questions, but it is well suited for problems involving clarification of perspective, opportunity, and hypotheses generation and a whole range of exploratory analyses. It is also useful as a tool for obtaining a better understanding of the results of more quantitative analyses based on formal survey research or experimentation. The opportunity for focus group participants to express opinions and ideas in their own words is a particularly attractive feature of focus groups. Another, and one virtually unique to them, is the fact that the group is itself a research instrument. The dynamic interaction of the group under the subtle but firm direction of a skilled moderator can yield insights not easily obtained by other means.

In addition to providing the theoretical foundations on which the focus group interview is based, we have also provided a description of how focus group research is carried out. Practical issues related to recruiting participants, designing the interview guide, analyzing data, and reporting results have been addressed, and an illustrative example of a focus group project was presented in the previous chapter. We have also provided a discussion of the process of conducting a group and of techniques that may be useful in dealing with various problems that may arise during the course of an interview.

This book is intended as a place to begin learning about focus group interviewing. Ultimately, the best teacher is experience. Like most other research tools, proficiency comes with practice. Individuals who wish to add focus groups to their set of research tools would do well to observe several groups under the direction of an experienced moderator before attempting them on their own. This provides an opportunity to see a variety of groups interact and the way the moderator handles specific problems as they arise. It also provides a means for reducing anxiety associated with moderating a group, because focus groups tend to be lively and fun, for participants *and* the moderator.

Throughout this book, we have drawn attention to the limitations of focus group interviews as well as to their advantages. We would be remiss if we did not once more draw attention to these limitations. Perhaps the greatest of the limitations associated with focus groups is that each group really represents a single observation. Simply because a dozen people are involved in a group discussion does not mean that there are 12 independent observations. By definition and by design, the statements of focus group participants are influenced by the group interaction and the opinions of others. As a result of this influence, as well as the fact that it is seldom the case that more than a few groups are conducted on any one topic, statistical estimation is not possible, nor is it appropriate to generalize about specific population parameters based on focus group results. This is not to say that all generalization is inappropriate. We would not carry out focus group research if it did not yield some insights about individuals beyond those who participate in the group discussion. Rather, the types of generalizations that arise from focus group results tend to be more general than specific, more tentative, and more descriptive.

Other limitations of focus groups tend to be similar to those of other research techniques that employ human beings. These include problems associated with nonrepresentative samples, interviewer bias, and demand effects. In the case of focus groups, the demand effects are likely to result from the composition of the group, the presence of a particularly dominant member of the group, the actions of the moderator, or some other group-related factor. Thus, focus groups share many of the same limitations as many other research tools, including survey research and experimentation. The sources of these limitations and problems may differ somewhat, but the problems are the same.

Throughout this book, we have suggested that the focus group interview is a powerful and useful tool when used appropriately and for the purposes for which it is intended. This is true of all research techniques. Ultimately, the true test of the validity of a research technique is determined by the frequency with which it yields useful, interesting, and actionable results. The persistence of the focus group interview for almost 50 years, its rapid growth as a tool for social science research, and the breadth of fields and applications to which it has been applied suggest that it has met this standard of validity.

References

Adams, G. R., & Huston, T. L. (1975). Social perception of middle-aged persons varying in physical attractiveness. *Developmental Psychology, 11,* 657–658.

Agar, M., & MacDonald, J. (1995). Focus groups and ethnography. *Human Organization, 54,* 78–86.

Allen, D. E., & Guy, R. F. (1977). Ocular breaks and verbal output. *Sociometry, 40,* 90–96.

Anderson, J. R. (1983). *The architecture of cognition.* Cambridge, MA: Harvard University Press.

Antworth, E., & Valentine, J. R. (1998). Software for doing field linguistics. In J. Lawler & H. A. Dry (Eds.), *Using computers in linguistics: A practical guide* (pp. 170–196). New York: Routledge.

Aries, E. (1976). Interaction patterns and themes of male, female, and mixed groups. *Small Group Behavior, 7,* 7–18.

Arnold, J. E. (1962). Useful creative techniques. In S. J. Parnes & H. F. Harding (Eds.), *Source book for creative thinking* (pp. 251–268). New York: Charles Scribner's Sons.

Ashmore, R. D., & Del Boca, F. K. (1981). Conceptual approaches to stereotypes and stereotyping. In D. L. Hamilton (Ed.), *Cognitive processes in stereotyping and intergroup behavior* (pp. 1–35). Hillsdale, NJ: Lawrence Erlbaum.

Axelrod, M. D. (1975, March 14). 10 essentials for good qualitative research. *Marketing News,* pp. 10–11.

Barabba, V. P. (1995). *Meeting of the minds.* Cambridge, MA: Harvard Business School Press.

Baxter, C. (1970). Interpersonal spacing in natural settings. *Sociometry, 33,* 444–456.

Beattie, G. W. (1978). Floor apportionment and gaze in conversational dyads. *British Journal of Sociology and Clinical Psychology, 17,* 7–15.

Beaver, A. P. (1932). *The initiation of social contacts by preschool children* (Child Development Monographs, No. 7). New York: Teachers College, Columbia University.

Bellenger, D. N., Bernhardt, K. L., & Goldstucker, J. L. (1976). *Qualitative research in marketing.* Chicago: American Marketing Association.

Berg, I. A., & Bass, B. M. (1961). *Conformity and deviation.* New York: Harper & Row.

Berkowitz, J. L. (1954). Group standards, cohesiveness, and productivity. *Human Relations, 7,* 509–519.

Bliss, J., Monk, M., & Ogborn, J. (1983). *Qualitative data analysis for educational research.* London: Groom Helm.

Bogardus, E. S. (1926). The group interview. *Journal of Applied Sociology, 10,* 372–382.

Bogdan, R. C., & Biklen, S. (1982). *Qualitative research for education.* Boston: Allyn & Bacon.

Bruner, J. S., Goodnow, J. J., & Austin, J. G. (1956). *A study of thinking.* New York: Wiley.

Bryant, A., & Emerson, T. (2000, June 5). Coffee, tea or . . . tennis? *Newsweek,* pp. 62–63.

Bryant, N. (1975). Petitioning: Dress congruence versus belief congruence. *Journal of Applied Social Psychology, 5,* 144–149.

Calder, B. J. (1977). Focus groups and the nature of qualitative marketing research. *Journal of Marketing Research, 14,* 353–364.

Carter, L. F. (1954). Recording and evaluating the performance of individuals as members of small groups. *Personnel Psychology, 7,* 477–484.

Cary, M. S. (1978). The role of gaze in the initiation of conversation. *Social Psychology, 41,* 269–271.

Costanzo, P. R., & Shaw, M. C. (1966). Conformity as a function of age level. *Child Development, 37,* 967–975.

Chaubey, N. P. (1974). Effect of age on expectancy of success on risk-taking behavior. *Journal of Personality and Social Psychology, 249,* 774–778.

Chemers, M. M. (2003). Leadership effectiveness: An integrative review. In M. A. Hogg & S. Tindale (Eds.), *Blackwell handbook of social psychology: Group processes* (pp. 376–399). Malden, MA: Blackwell.

Chomsky, N. (1965). *Aspects of the theory of syntax.* Cambridge: MIT Press.

Churchill, G., & Iacobucci, D. (2004). *Marketing research: Methodological foundations* (9th ed.). Mason, OH: South-Western.

Cohen, J. (1956). Experimental effects of ego-defense preference on relations. *Journal of Abnormal and Social Psychology, 52,* 19–27.

Dalkey, N. C., & Helmer, O. (1963). An experimental application of the Delphi method to the use of experts. *Management Science, 9,* 458.

Deaux, K., & Lafrance, M. (1998). Gender. In D. T. Gilbert, S. T. Fiske, & G. Lindzey (Eds.), *The handbook of social psychology* (4th ed., Vol. 1, pp. 788–827). New York: McGraw-Hill.

Delbecq, A. L., Van de Ven, A., & Gustafson, H. (1975). Guidelines for conducting NGT meetings. In A. L. Delbecq, A. H. Van de Ven, & D. H. Gustafson (Eds.), *Group techniques for program planning* (pp. 40–66). Glenview, IL: Scott, Foresman.

DePaulo, B. M., Rosenthal, V., Eisentat, R. A., Rogers, P. L., & Finkelstein, S. (1978). Decoding discrepant nonverbal cues. *Journal of Personality and Social Psychology, 36,* 313–323.

Dichter, E. (1947). Psychology in marketing research. *Harvard Business Review, 25,* 432–443.

Duriau, V. J., & Reger, R. K. (2004). Choice of text analysis software in organization research: Insight from a multi-dimensional scaling (MDS) analysis. *JADT 2004: 7es Journées internationales d'Analyse statistique des Données Textuelles, 7,* 382–389.

Dymond, R. S., Hughes, A. S., & Raabe, V. L. (1952). Measurable changes in empathy with age. *Journal of Consulting Psychology, 16,* 202–206.

Dyson, J. W., Godwin, P. H. B., & Hazelwood, L. A. (1976). Group composition, leadership, orientation, and decisional outcomes. *Small Group Behavior, 7,* 114–128.

Edmiston, V. (1944, April). The group interview. *Journal of Educational Research, 37,* 593–601.

Edmunds, H. (1999). *Focus group research handbook.* Chicago: American Marketing Association.

Ellsworth, P. C., Friedman, H. S., Perlick, E., & Hoyt, M. E. (1978). Some effects of gaze on subjects motivated to seek or to avoid social comparison. *Journal of Experimental Social Psychology, 14,* 69–87.

Emerson, R. M. (1964). Power-dependence relations: Two experiments. *Sociometry, 27,* 282–298.

Fern, E. (1982). The use of focus groups for idea generation: The effects of group size, acquaintanceship, and moderator on response quantity and quality. *Journal of Marketing Research, 19,* 1–13.

Fern, E. (2001). *Advanced focus group research.* Thousand Oaks, CA: Sage.

Fiedler, F. E. (1967). *A theory of leadership effectiveness.* New York: McGraw-Hill.

Finkle, R. (1976). Managerial assessment centers. In M. Dunnette (Ed.), *Handbook of industrial and organizational psychology* (pp. 861–888). Chicago: Rand McNally.

Fiske, S. T. (1998). Stereotyping, prejudice, and discrimination. In D. T. Gilbert, S. T. Fiske, & G. Lindzey (Eds.), *The handbook of social psychology* (4th ed., Vol. 2, pp. 357–411). New York: McGraw-Hill.

Forsyth, D. R. (2006). *Group dynamics* (rev. ed.). Belmont, CA: Wadsworth.

Fowler, F. J., Jr. (2002). *Survey research methods* (3rd ed.). Thousand Oaks, CA: Sage.

Fowler, F. J., Jr., & Mangione, T. W. (1989). *Standardized survey interviewing.* Newbury Park, CA: Sage.

French, J. R. P., Jr., & Raven, B. (1959). The bases of social power. In D. Cartwright (Ed.), *Studies in social power* (pp. 150–167). Ann Arbor, MI: Institute for Social Research.

Frieze, I. (1980). Being male or female. In P. Middlebrook (Ed.), *Social psychology and modern life* (2nd ed., pp. 80-115). New York: Alfred A. Knopf.

Fry, C. L. (1965). Personality and acquisition factors in the development of coordination strategy. *Journal of Personality and Social Psychology, 2,* 403–407.

Gallup, G. (1947). The quintamensional plan of question design. *Public Opinion Quarterly, 11,* 385.

Gibbins, K. (1969). Communication aspects of women's clothes and their relation to fashion ability. *British Journal of Social and Clinical Psychology, 8,* 301–312.

Gladwell, M. (2005). *Blink: The power of thinking without thinking.* New York: Little, Brown.

Goldman, A. E. (1962). The group depth interview. *Journal of Marketing, 26,* 61–68.

Goldman, A. E., & McDonald, S. S. (1987). *The group depth interview: Principles and practice.* Englewood Cliffs, NJ: Prentice Hall.

Goldman, W., & Lewis, P. (1977). Beautiful is good: Evidence that the physically attractive are more socially skillful. *Journal of Experimental Social Psychology, 13,* 125–130.

Gottschalk, L. A., Winget, C. N., & Gleser, G. C. (1969). *Manual of instructions for using the Gottschalk-Gleser Content Analysis Scales.* Berkeley: University of California Press.

Greenbaum, T. L. (2000). *Moderating focus groups: A practical guide for group facilitation.* Thousand Oaks, CA: Sage.

Grunert, K. G. (1982). Linear processing in a semantic network: An alternative view of consumer product evaluation. *Journal of Business Research, 10,* 31–42.

Grunert, K. G., & Goder, M. (1986, August). *A systematic way to analyze focus group data.* Paper presented to the 1986 Summer Marketing Educator's Conference of the American Marketing Association, Chicago.

Hahn, U., & Ramscar, M. (2001). *Similarity and categorization.* New York: Oxford University Press.

Hall, J. A. (1978). Gender effects in decoding nonverbal cues. *Psychological Bulletin, 85,* 845–857.

Hall, J. A. (1980). Voice tone and persuasion. *Journal of Personality and Social Psychology, 38,* 924–934.

Hare, A. P., & Bales, R. F. (1963). Seating position and small group interaction. *Sociometry, 26,* 480–486.

Haythorn, W. W., Couch, A., Haefner, D., Langham, P., & Carter, L. F. (1956). The behavior of authoritarian and equalitarian personalities in groups. *Human Relations, 9,* 57–74.

Henderson, N. (2004, Summer). Same frame, new game. *Marketing Research, 16,* 38–39.

Hess, J. M. (1968). Group interviewing. In R. L. Ring (Ed.), *New science of planning.* Chicago: American Marketing Association.

Higgenbotham, J. B., & Cox, K. K. (Eds.). (1979). *Focus group interviews: A reader.* Chicago: American Marketing Association.

Hoffman, L. R. (1959). Homogeneity of member personality and its effect on group problem-solving. *Journal of Abnormal Behavior and Psychology, 58,* 27–32.

Hoffman, L. R., & Maier, N. R. F. (1961). Quality and acceptance of problem solutions by members of homogeneous and heterogeneous groups. *Journal of Abnormal Behavior and Social Psychology, 62,* 401–407.

Hollander, J. A. (2004). The social context of focus groups. *Journal of Contemporary Ethnography, 33,* 602–637.

Hollingshead, A. (2003). Communication technologies: The Internet and group research. In M. A. Hogg & S. Tindale (Eds.), *Blackwell handbook of social psychology: Group processes* (pp. 557–573). Malden, MA: Blackwell.

House, R. J., & Baetz, M. L. (1979). Leadership: Some empirical generalizations and research directions. In B. M. Staw (Ed.), *Research in organizational behavior* (pp. 341–423). Greenwich, CT: JAI.

House, R. J., & Mitchell, T. R. (1974). Path-goal theory of leadership. *Journal of Contemporary Business, 3,* 81–97.

Hurwitz, J. I., Zander, A. F., & Hymovitch, B. (1953). Some effects of power on the relations among group members. In D. Cartwright & A. Zander (Eds.), *Group dynamics: research and theory* (pp. 483–492). Evanston, IL: Row, Peterson.

Ivy, D. K., & Backlund, P. (1994). *Exploring gender speak: Personal effectiveness in gender communication.* New York: McGraw-Hill.

Janis, I. L. (1965). The problem of validating content analysis. In H. D. Lasswell et al. (Eds.), *Language of politics* (pp. 55–82). Cambridge: MIT Press.

Jones, R. A. (1977). *Self-fulfilling prophecies: Social, psychological and physiological effects of expectancies.* Hillsdale, NJ: Lawrence Erlbaum.

Karger, T. (1987, August 28). Focus groups are for focusing, and for little else. *Marketing News,* pp. 52–55.

Kassarjian, H. H. (1994). Scholarly traditions and European roots of American consumer research. In G. Laurent, G. Lilien, & B. Pras (Eds.), *Research traditions in marketing* (pp. 265–287). Boston: Kluwer Academic.

Kaufman, L. (1997, August 18). Enough talk. *Newsweek,* pp. 48–49.

Kendon, A. (1978). Looking in conversation and the regulation of turns at talk: A comment on the papers of G. Beattie & D. R. Rutter et al. *British Journal of Sociology and Clinical Psychology, 17,* 23–24.

Kennedy, F. (1976, February-March). The focused group interview and moderator bias. *Marketing Review, 31,* 19–21.

Kidd, P. S., & Parshall, M. B. (2000, May). Getting the focus and the group: Enhancing analytical rigor in focus group research. *Qualitative Health Research, 10,* 293–308.

Kiley, D. (2005, November 14). Shoot the focus group. *BusinessWeek,* pp. 120–121.

Krauss, R. M., Garlock, C. M., Bricker, P. D., & McMahon, L. E. (1977). The role of audible and visible back-channel responses in interpersonal communication. *Journal of Personality and Social Psychology, 35,* 523–529.

Krippendorf, K. (1970). Bivariate agreement coefficients for reliability data. In E. F. Borgatta & G. W. Bohrnstedt (Eds.), *Sociological methodology* (pp. 139–150). San Francisco: Jossey-Bass.

Krippendorf, K. (2004). *Content analysis: An introduction to its methodology* (2nd ed.). Thousand Oaks, CA: Sage.

Krueger, R. A., & Casey, M. A. (2000). *Focus groups: A practical guide for applied research* (3rd ed.). Thousand Oaks, CA: Sage.

Langer, J. (1978, September 8). Clients: Check qualitative researcher's personal traits to get more. Qualitative researchers: Enter entire marketing process to give more. *Marketing News,* pp. 10–11.

Lazarsfeld, P. F. (1934, October). The psychological aspects of market research. *Harvard Business Review, 13,* 54–71.

Lazarsfeld, P. F. (1937, July). The use of detailed interviews in market research. *Journal of Marketing, 2,* 3–8.

Lecuyer, R. (1975). Space dimensions, the climate of discussion and group decisions. *European Journal of Social Psychology, 46,* 38–50.

Leonhard, D. (1967). *The human equation in marketing research.* New York: American Management Association.

Levine, J. M., & Moreland, R. L. (1998). Small groups. In D. T. Gilbert, S. T. Fiske, & G. Lindzey (Eds.), *The handbook of social psychology* (4th ed., Vol. 2, pp. 415–469). New York: McGraw-Hill.

Levy, S. J. (1979). Focus group interviewing. In J. B. Higginbotham & K. K. Cox (Eds.), *Focus group interviews: A reader* (pp. 34–42). Chicago: American Marketing Association.

Lewin, K. (1948). *Resolving social conflicts.* New York: Harper.

Linstone, H. A., & Turoff, M. (1975). *The Delphi method: Techniques and applications.* Reading, MA: Addison-Wesley.

Lippitt, R., Polansky, N., Redl, F., & Rosen, S. (1952). The dynamics of power. *Human Relations, 5,* 37–64.

Little, K. B. (1965). Personal space. *Journal of Experimental Social Psychology, 1,* 237–257.

Lorr, M., & McNair, D. M. (1966). Methods relating to evaluation of therapeutic outcome. In L. A. Gottschalk & A. H. Auerbach (Eds.), *Methods of research in psychotherapy* (pp. 573–594). Englewood Cliffs, NJ: Prentice Hall.

Lott, D. F., & Sommer, R. (1967). Seating arrangements and status. *Journal of Personality and Social Psychology, 7,* 90–95.

Lunt, P., & Livingstone, S. (1996). Rethinking the focus group in media and communications research. *Journal of Communication, 46,* 79–98.

Maier, N. R. F., & Hoffman, L. R. (1961). Organization and creative problem solving. *Journal of Applied Psychology, 45,* 277–280.

Mannheim, K. (1936). *Ideology and utopia: An introduction to the sociology of knowledge.* New York: Harcourt Brace.

Mariampolski, H. (2001). *Qualitative market research.* Thousand Oaks, CA: Sage.

McCracken, G. (1988). *The long interview.* Newbury Park, CA: Sage.

McGrath, J. E., & Kravitz, D. A. (1982). Group research. *Annual Review of Psychology, 33,* 195–230.

McQuarrie, E. F., & Mick, D. G. (1996). Figures of rhetoric in advertising language. *Journal of Consumer Research, 22,* 424–438.

Medin, D. I., Lynch, E. B., & Solomon, K. O. (2000). Are there kinds of concepts? *Annual Review of Psychology, 51,* 121–147.

Mehrabian, A., & Diamond, S. G. (1971). Effects of furniture arrangement, props, and personality on social interaction. *Journal of Personality and Social Psychology, 20,* 18–30.

Meisels, M., & Guardo, C. J. (1969). Development of personal space schemata. *Child Development, 40,* 1167–1178.

Merton, R. K. (1987). Focussed interviews and focus groups: Continuities and discontinuities. *Public Opinion Quarterly, 51,* 550–566.

Merton, R. K., Fiske, M., & Curtis, P. L. (1946). *Mass persuasion.* New York: Harper & Row.

Merton, R. K., Fiske, M., & Kendall, P. L. (1956). *The focussed interview.* New York: Free Press.

Merton, R. K., & Kendall, P. L. (1946). The focussed interview. *American Journal of Sociology, 51,* 541–557.

Miller, D. T., & Turnbull, W. (1986). Expectancies and interpersonal processes. *Annual Review of Psychology, 37,* 233–256.

Mohler, P. Ph., & Zuell, C. (1998). *TEXTPACK: Short description*. Mannheim, Germany: ZUMA.

Moore, C. M. (1987). *Group techniques for idea building*. Newbury Park, CA: Sage.

Moreno, J. L. (1931). *The first book on group psychotherapy*. New York: Beacon House.

Morgan, D. L. (1996). Focus groups. In J. Hagan & K. S. Cook (Eds.), *Annual Review of Sociology* (Vol. 22, pp. 129–152). Palo Alto, CA: Annual Reviews.

Morgan, D. L. (1997). *Focus groups as qualitative research* (2nd ed.). Thousand Oaks, CA: Sage.

Morgan, D. L. (1998). *Planning focus groups*. Thousand Oaks, CA: Sage.

Morgan, D. L., & Spanish, M. T. (1984). Focus groups: A new tool for qualitative research. *Qualitative Sociology, 7*, 253–270.

Napier, R. W., & Gershenfeld, M. K. (2003). *Groups: Theory and experience* (7th ed.). Mahwah, NJ: Lawrence Erlbaum.

Nelems, J. (2003, February). Qualitatively speaking: The focus group—popular but dangerous. *Quirks Marketing Research Review*. Retrieved August 23, 2004, from http://www.quirks.com/articles/article.asp?arg_ArticleId=1086

Neuendorf, K. A. (2002). *The content analysis guidebook*. Thousand Oaks, CA: Sage.

Osborn, A. F. (1963). *Applied imagination* (3rd ed.). New York: Charles Scribner's Sons.

Patterson, M. L., & Schaeffer, R. E. (1977). Effects of size and sex composition on interaction distance, participation, and satisfaction in small groups. *Small Group Behavior, 8*, 433–442.

Payne, S. (1951). *The art of asking questions*. Princeton, NJ: Princeton University Press.

Pennington, D. C. (2002). *The social psychology of behaviour in small groups*. New York: Taylor & Francis.

Peters, L. H., Hartke, D. D., & Pohlmann, J. T. (1985). Fielder's contingency theory of leadership: An application of the meta-analysis procedure of Schmidt and Hunter. *Psychological Bulletin, 97*, 274–285.

Piaget, J. (1954). *The moral judgment of the child*. New York: Basic Books.

Poffenberger, A. T. (1925). *Psychology in advertising*. Chicago: A. W. Shaw.

Pollack, J. (2005, December 19). Those who made their mark. *Advertising Age*, p. 8.

Popping, R. (2002). *Computer-assisted text analysis*. Thousand Oaks, CA: Sage.

Provalis Research. (2005). *WORDSTAT v4.0: Content analysis and text mining module for Simstat and QDA Miner*. Montreal: Provalis Research.

Qualitative Research Counsel. (1985). *Focus groups: Issues and approaches*. New York: Advertising Research Foundation.

Quiriconi, R. J., & Durgan, R. E. (1985). Respondent personalities: Insight for better focus groups. *Journal of Data Collection, 25*, 20–23.

Reid, N. L., Soley, N., & Wimmer, R. D. (1980). Replication in advertising research. *Journal of Advertising, 9*, 3–13.

Reitan, H. T., & Shaw, M. E. (1964). Group membership, sex-composition of the group, and conformity behavior. *Journal of Social Psychology, 64*, 45–51.

Reynolds, F. D., & Johnson, D. K. (1978). Validity of focus-group findings. *Journal of Advertising Research, 18*, 21–24.

Rook, D. W. (2003, Summer). Out-of-focus groups. *Marketing Research, 15*(2), 11.

Ruhe, J. A. (1972). *The effects of varying racial compositions upon attitudes and behavior of supervisors and subordinates in simulated work groups.* Unpublished doctoral dissertation, University of Florida, Gainesville.

Ruhe, J. A. (1978). Effect of leader sex and leader behavior on group problem solving. *Proceedings of the American Institute for Decision Sciences, Northeast Division,* May, 123–127.

Ruhe, J. A., & Allen, W. R. (1977, April). Differences and similarities between black and white leaders. *Proceedings of the American Institute for Decision Sciences, Northeast Division,* 30–35.

Rutter, D. R., & Stephenson, G. M. (1979). The functions of looking: Effects of friendship on gaze. *British Journal of Social and Clinical Psychology, 18,* 203–205.

Rutter, D. R., Stephenson, G. M., Ayling, K., & White, P. A. (1978). The timing of looks in dyadic conversation. *British Journal of Social and Clinical Psychology, 17,* 17–21.

Sapir, E. (1929). The status of linguistics as a science. *Language, 5,* 207–214.

Sapolsky, A. (1960). Effect of interpersonal relationships upon verbal conditioning. *Journal of Abnormal and Social Psychology, 60,* 241–246.

Sayre, S. (2001). *Qualitative methods for marketplace research.* Thousand Oaks, CA: Sage.

Schachter, S. N., Ellertson, N., McBride, D., & Gregory, D. (1951). An experimental study of cohesiveness and productivity. *Human Relations, 4,* 229–238.

Schaeffer, N. C., & Presser, S. (2003). The science of asking questions. *Annual Review of Sociology, 29,* 65–88.

Schoenfeld, G. (1988, May 23). Unfocus and learn more. *Advertising Age,* p. 20.

Schutz, A. (1967). *The phenomenology of the social world.* Evanston, IL: Northwestern University Press.

Schutz, W. C. (1958). *FIRO: A three dimensional theory of interpersonal behavior.* New York: Rinehart.

Scott, D. N. (1987, Aug. 28). Good focus group session needs the touch of an artist. *Marketing News,* 35.

Scott, W. A. (1955). Reliability of content analysis: The case of nominal coding. *Public Opinion Quarterly, 19,* 321–325.

Shaw, M. E. (1981). *Group dynamics: The psychology of small group behavior* (3rd ed.). New York: McGraw-Hill.

Shaw, M. E., & Shaw, L. M. (1962). Some effects of sociometric grouping upon learning in a second grade classroom. *Journal of Social Psychology, 57,* 453–458.

Sherif, M., & Sherif, C. W. (1969). *Social psychology.* New York: Harper & Row.

Smelser, W. T. (1961). Dominance as a factor in achievement and perception in cooperative problem solving interactions. *Journal of Abnormal and Social Psychology, 62,* 535–542.

Smith, G. H. (1954). *Motivation research in advertising and marketing.* New York: McGraw-Hill.

Smith, K. H. (1977). Small-group interaction at various ages: Simultaneous talking and interruption of others. *Small Group Behavior, 8,* 65–74.

Smith, R. G. (1978). *The message measurement inventory: A profile for communication analysis.* Bloomington: Indiana University Press.

Snyder, M. (1984). When belief creates reality. *Advances in Experimental Social Psychology, 18*, 62–113.

Snyder, M., & Cantor, N. (1998). Understanding personality and social behavior: A functionalist strategy. In D. T. Gilbert, S. T. Fiske, & G. Lindzey (Eds.), *The handbook of social psychology* (4th ed., Vol. 1, pp. 635–679). New York: McGraw-Hill.

Social Science Consulting. (2005). *TextQuest: Software for text analysis.* Rudolstadt, Germany: Author.

Sommer, R. (1959). Studies in personal space. *Sociometry, 22*, 247–260.

Spiegelman, M. C., Terwilliger, C., & Fearing, F. (1953). The reliability of agreement in content analysis. *Journal of Social Psychology, 37*, 175–187.

Steinzor, B. (1950). The spatial factor in face-to-face discussion groups. *Journal of Abnormal and Social Psychology, 45*, 552–555.

Stern, B. (1995). Consumer myths: Frye's taxonomy and the structural analysis of consumption text. *Journal of Consumer Research, 22*, 165–185.

Stewart, C. J., & Cash, W. B. (2002). *Interviewing: Principles and practices* (10th ed.). New York: McGraw-Hill.

Stewart, D. W., & Shamdasani, P. (1990). *Focus groups: Theory and research.* Newbury Park, CA: Sage.

Stewart, D. W., & Shamdasani, P. (1992). Analytical issues in focus group research. *Asian Journal of Marketing, 1*(1), 27–42.

Stewart, D. W., & Shamdasani, P. (1997). Focus group research: Exploration and discovery. In L. Bickman & D. Rog (Eds.), *Handbook of applied social research methods* (pp. 505–526). Thousand Oaks, CA: Sage.

Stogdill, R. M. (1948). Personal factors associated with leadership: A survey of the literature. *Journal of Psychology, 25*, 35–71.

Stogdill, R. M. (1950). Leadership, membership and organization. *Psychological Bulletin, 47*, 1–14.

Stogdill, R. M. (1974). *Handbook of leadership: A survey of theory and research.* New York: Free Press.

Stogdill, R. M., & Coons, A. E. (Eds.). (1957). *Leader behavior: Its description and measurement.* Columbus: Ohio State University, Bureau of Business Research.

Stone, P. J., Dunphy, D. C., Smith, M. S., & Ogilvie, D. M. (1966). *The general inquirer: A computer approach to content analysis.* Cambridge: MIT Press.

Stone, P. J., & Hunt, E. B. (1963). A computer approach to content analysis using the general inquirer system. In E. C. Johnson (Ed.), *Conference Proceedings of the American Federation of Information Processing Societies*, 241–256.

Strodbeck, F. L., & Hook, L. H. (1961). The social dimensions of a twelve-man jury table. *Sociometry, 24*, 397–415.

Strong, E. K., Jr. (1913). Psychological methods as applied to advertising. *Journal of Educational Psychology, 4*, 393–395.

Sudman, S., & Bradburn, N. M. (1982). *Asking questions.* San Francisco: Jossey-Bass.

Swim, J. K., & Campbell, B. (2003). Sexism: Attitudes, beliefs, and behaviors. In R. Brown & S. Gaertner (Eds.), *Blackwell handbook of social psychology: Intergroup processes* (pp. 218–237). Malden, MA: Blackwell.

Tannenbaum, R., Weschler, I. R., & Massarik, F. (1961). *Leadership and organization: A behavioral science approach.* New York: McGraw-Hill.

Templeton, J. F. (1994). *The focus group: A strategic guide to organizing, conducting and analyzing the focus group interview* (2nd ed.). New York: McGraw-Hill.

Tennis, G. H., & Dabbs, J. M., Jr. (1975). Sex, setting and personal space: First grade through college. *Sociometry, 38,* 385–394.

Thompson, C. (1997). Interpreting consumers: A hermeneutic framework for deriving marketing insights from the texts of consumers' consumption stories. *Journal of Marketing Research, 34,* 438–455.

Torrance, E. P. (1954). Some consequences of power differences on decision making in permanent and temporary three-man groups. *Research Studies, 22,* 130–140.

Umiker-Sebeok, J. (Ed.). (1987). *Marketing and semiotics: New directions for the study of signs for sale.* Berlin: Walter de Gruyter.

Van Zelst, R. H. (1952a). Sociometrically selected work teams increase production. *Personnel Psychology, 5,* 175–186.

Van Zelst, R. H. (1952b). Validation of a sociometric regrouping procedure. *Journal of Abnormal and Social Psychology, 47,* 299–301.

Vaughn, S., Schumm, J. S., & Singagub, J. (1996). *Focus group interviews in education and psychology.* Thousand Oaks, CA: Sage.

Watson, D., & Bromberg, B. (1965). Power, communication, and position satisfaction in task-oriented groups. *Journal of Personality and Social Psychology, 2,* 859–864.

Watt, R. J. C. (2004). *Concordance: Manual for version 3.2.* Dundee, UK: Concordance Software.

Wellner, A. (2003, March 1). The new science of focus groups. *American Demographics,* pp. 29–33.

Wells, W. D. (1974). Group interviewing. In R. Ferber (Ed.), *Handbook of marketing research* (pp. 133–147). New York: McGraw-Hill.

Wheatley, K. L., & Flexner, W. A. (1988, May 9). Dimensions that make focus group work. *Marketing News, 22,* 16–17.

Willis, F. N., Jr. (1966). Initial speaking distance as a function of the speakers' relationship. *Psychonomic Science, 5,* 221–222.

Yukl, G. A. (1981). *Leadership in organizations.* Englewood Cliffs, NJ: Prentice Hall.

Zaltman, G. (1989). *The use of developmental and evaluative market research* (Report no. 89–107). Cambridge, MA: Marketing Science Institute.

Zaltman, G. (2003). *How customers think.* Boston: Harvard Business School Press.

Zander, A., & Cohen, A. R. (1955). Attributed social power and group acceptance: A classroom experimental demonstration. *Journal of Abnormal and Social Psychology, 51,* 490–492.

Index

About the Authors

David W. Stewart is the Robert E. Brooker Professor of Marketing at the Marshall School of Business at the University of Southern California. He is a past Editor of the *Journal of Marketing* and has authored or coauthored more than 200 publications, including seven books. His research has examined a wide range of issues including marketing strategy, the analysis of markets, consumer information search and decision making, effectiveness of marketing communications, public policy issues related to marketing, and methodological approaches to the analysis of marketing data. His research and commentary are frequently featured in the business and popular press. In 2006, he received the Academy of Marketing Science Distinguished Marketing Educator Award. He has also been honored for innovation in teaching by the Decision Sciences Institute, and in 1996, he was a member of a four-person faculty team honored by the U.S. Distance Learning Association for the "Best Distance Learning Program 1996—Continuing Education." In 1998, he received the American Academy of Advertising award for Outstanding Contribution to Advertising Research. His paper on warning messages was named the best paper published in the *Journal of Public Policy and Marketing* during 1992–1994, and he was recipient of the American Academy of Advertising Award for best paper in the *Journal of Advertising* in 1989. In 1988, he was Marketing Science Institute Visiting Scholar at the General Motors Corporation. He has been included in *Who's Who in America, Who's Who of the World, Who's Who in American Education,* and *Who's Who in Advertising.* His experience includes work as a manager of research for Needham, Harper, and Steers Advertising (now DDB), Chicago, and consulting projects for a wide range of organizations. A native of Baton Rouge, Louisiana, he received his BA from the Northeast Louisiana University (now the University of Louisiana at Monroe) and his MA and PhD in psychology from Baylor University.

Prem N. Shamdasani is Associate Professor of Marketing, Director of the Commonwealth-Singapore Chief Executives Program and Co-Director of the Stanford-NUS and Berkeley-NUS Executive Programs at the National University of Singapore. He was the former Director of the Master of Science (Marketing) Program and Director of the Office of Executive Education (English) at the NUS Business School, National University of Singapore. He holds a First Class Honors BBA degree from the National University of Singapore and received his PhD from the University of Southern California. His research and teaching interests include brand management, new product marketing, retail strategy, relationship marketing, and cross-cultural consumer behavior.

He has taught in the United States and has received numerous commendations for teaching excellence. Aside from teaching graduate and executive MBA courses, he is very active in executive development and training for such clients as Caterpillar, Johnson & Johnson, Nokia, Samsung, Dupont, Asahi Glass, Philips, Siemens, Telenor, Exel, Royal Brunei Airlines, Singapore Airlines, GlaxoSmithKline, DaimlerChrysler, Ikea, Carrefour, Royal Ahold, NTUC Fairprice, Danone, Ceylinco, Singapore Tourism Board, National Service Affairs Department, Ministry of Foreign Affairs, and Commonwealth Secretariat (UK). He is actively involved in focus group research for consumer products companies and social marketing programs. His research publications have appeared in the leading regional and international journals, including the *Journal of Consumer Research, European Journal of Marketing, Journal of Advertising Research, Asian Journal of Marketing, Asia Pacific Journal of Management,* and *Journal of Retailing and Consumer Services.*

Dennis W. Rook is a Professor of Clinical Marketing at the Marshall School of Business at the University of Southern California. He received his PhD in marketing in 1983 from Northwestern University's Kellogg Graduate School of Management, where he concentrated in consumer behavior theory and qualitative research methods. Following this, he served on the marketing faculty of the University of Southern California in Los Angeles. He left the academic environment in 1987 to join the Strategic Planning Department of DDB Needham Worldwide in Chicago, where he was a research supervisor. Following this, he was appointed Director of Qualitative Research Services at Conway/Milliken & Associates, a Chicago research and consulting company. He rejoined the USC marketing faculty in 1991. His published research has investigated consumer impulse buying, "solo" consumption behavior, and consumers' buying rituals and fantasies. These and other studies have appeared in the *Journal of Consumer Research, Advances in Consumer Research, Symbolic Consumer Behavior,* and *Research in Consumer Behavior.* He has served as Treasurer of the Association for Consumer Research, for which he is also a member of the Advisory Council. In 1985, his dissertation research was awarded by the Association for Consumer Research, and in 1988, he was appointed to the Editorial Board of the *Journal of Consumer Research.* He has served as a research and marketing consultant for companies in the consumer packaged goods, financial services, communications, and entertainment industries.